Volume 18, Number 4, 2017

Quarterly Review
OF Distance
Education

RESEARCH THAT GUIDES PRACTICE

Editors:
Michael Simonson
Charles Schlosser

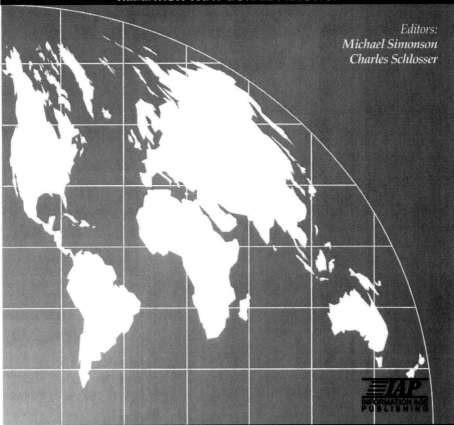

An Official Journal of the
Association for Educational Communications and Technology

Quarterly Review of Distance Education
"Research That Guides Practice"
Volume 18, Number 4, 2017

ARTICLES

STATEMENT OF PURPOSE

The *Quarterly Review of Distance Education* is a rigorously refereed journal publishing articles, research briefs, reviews, and editorials dealing with the theories, research, and practices of distance education. The *Quarterly Review* publishes articles that utilize various methodologies that permit generalizable results which help guide the practice of the field of distance education in the public and private sectors. The *Quarterly Review* publishes full-length manuscripts as well as research briefs, editorials, reviews of programs and scholarly works, and columns. The *Quarterly Review* defines distance education as institutionally based, formal education, where the learning group is separated and where interactive technologies are used to unite the learning group.

DIRECTIONS TO CONTRIBUTORS

Submit four copies of your manuscript, typed double-spaced on 8½ × 11 paper. Manuscripts should be between 10 and 30 pages in length and must conform to the style of the *Publication Manual of the American Psychological Association* (6th ed.). Research Briefs may be shorter, normally between 3 and 10 pages.

The name(s), affiliation(s), address(es), phone numbers, e-mail address(es), and a brief biography of the author(s) should appear on a separate cover page. To ensure anonymity in the review process, names of author(s) should not appear elsewhere in the manuscript, except in appropriate citations. An abstract of 100 words should also be submitted and typed on a separate page.

Printed documents should also be submitted on a flash drive using a recent version of Microsoft Word. The drive should be clearly labeled with the author(s) name(s) and name and version of the word processing program used. Also include an RTF version of the document. Graphics should be in a separate file, clearly labeled, not included as part of the Word document.

Manuscripts will be reviewed by at least three consulting editors. This process normally takes from 3-4 months.

Submit manuscripts to:

Michael Simonson
Charles Schlosser
Editors
Fischler College of Education
Nova Southeastern University
3301 College Avenue
Fort Lauderdale, FL 33314
simsmich@nova.edu

Name of Publication: *Quarterly Review of Distance Education*
(ISSN: 1528-3518)
Issue: Volume 18, Number 4, 2017
Frequency: Quarterly

Office of Publication: IAP–Information Age Publishing, Inc.
P.O. Box 79049
Charlotte, NC 28271-7047
Tel: 704-752-9125
Fax: 704-752-9113
E-mail: QRDE@infoagepub.com
Web Address: www.infoagepub.com

Subscription Rates:

Institutions Print: $200.00
Personal Print: $95.00
Student Print: $65.00

Single Issue Price (print only): Institutions: $45.00, Personal $25.00
Back Issue Special Price (print only): Institutions $100.00;
Personal: $50.00; Student: $35.00
Outside the U.S. please add $25.00 for surface mail.

Editorial Office: *Quarterly Review of Distance Education*
Department of Higher Education Leadership
and Instructional Technology
Fischler College of Education
Nova Southeastern University
3301 College Avenue
Fort Lauderdale, FL 33314
800-986-3223 ext. 8563
simsmich@nova.edu

Quarterly Review of Distance Education is indexed
by the DE Hub Database of Distance Education.

MAKING STUDENT ONLINE TEAMS WORK

Joel Olson and Ray Kalinski
Purdue University Global

Online professors typically assign teams based on time zones, performance, or alphabet, but are these the best ways to position student virtual teams for success? Personality and task complexity could provide additional direction. Personality and task complexity were used as independent variables related to the dependent variable of team performance. Four hundred-fifty students starting an MBA in a proprietary online university took the Insights Discovery (ID) personality assessment. Students were randomly assigned to 138 teams. Each team had 3 deliverables, which were ranked using the Bonner Model of Task Complexity (Bonner, 1994). Performance was determined by the grade given by the professor. Teams were designated as Variable when all ID personality types were present and Dominant when 50% or more of the team members had one ID personality type. Using ID, teams were also categorized as extroverted/introverted or thinking/feeling. *T* tests and ANOVAs were used to determine statistical difference. Extroverted teams outperformed introverted teams and Variable (heterogeneous) teams outperformed Dominant (homogeneous) teams with complex tasks.

INTRODUCTION

Team projects play an important role with online classes (Palloff & Pratt, 1999; Williams & Castro, 2010). Seung (2006) highlighted the progress of virtual teams in online education. However, the virtual environment of online courses creates obstacles for compatibility and group interaction (Hewson & Hughes, 2005; McInnerney & Roberts, 2004). Carver and Kosloski (2015) pointed out that, "online teachers and course developers must find ways to encourage students to work in teams and communicate during online course" (p. 17). Professors are not always sure how to create teams that feature the collaboration, creativity and problem solving required to be successful (Goold, Crain, & Coldwell, 2008).

One way of increasing collaboration, and the probability of success with student online teams, is to look at the relationship of personality type and team performance (Hewson & Hughes, 2005; Kline & O'Grady, 2009; McInnerney & Roberts, 2004). The findings have not been consistent (Barry & Stewart, 1997; Kline, 1999; Taggar, 2000; van Vianen & de Dreu, 2001; Yeatts & Hyten, 1998). Team performance and personality have been shown to be related in some studies (MacDonnell, O'Neill, Kline, & Hambley, 2009; Potter & Balthazard, 2002; Straus, 1996; Topi, Valacich, & Roe, 2002) and inconclusive in

• **Joel Olson**, PhD, Purdue University Global. E-mail: jolson@purdueglobal.edu

ISSN 1528-3518

others (Beise, Carte, Vician, & Chidambaram, 2010; Chantal, Beatrice & Peoll, 2010; Driskell, Hogan, & Salas, 1998; Faizuniah & Chan, 2014; Hackman & Morris, 1975; Moreland & Levine, 1992; Rutti, Ramsey, & Li, 2012).

A previous study by this group with the same sample reviewed the relationship between personality and virtual team performance (Olson, Ringhand, Kalinsky, & Ziegler, 2015). The study did not indicate that personality was a factor in team performance. No personality type or any combination of personality types, resulting in either heterogeneous or homogeneous teams, had a statistical impact on performance. There did appear to be a statistical difference with personality type and performance of increasingly complex tasks, which resulted in this follow-up study.

Task complexity may open a window to better understand the relationship between personality type and team performance. Not all tasks are the same and some personality types may be better suited to one level of task complexity than another. Additional research exploring this relationship could lead to an increased understanding of virtual team performance. Virtual teams could then be paired by personality type and task complexity to increase performance.

LITERATURE REVIEW

Task Definition and Characteristics

While tasks are a critical part of the human experience, there has not been consensus of its definition or characteristics (Hackman, 1969). Task characteristics can include task type, time to complete tasks, and who is assigned the task (Hackman & Oldham, 1976). Early research by Hackman (1968) and later by Hackman and Oldham (1976) defined task types characterized by production, discussion, and problem-Solving (Hackman, 1968). Production was defined as the development of ideas, discussion as the identification of values that result in-group consensus, and problem solving as

working to find a solution within a set of specified parameters.

Researchers have also classified tasks using multiple methods and characteristics. Bolt, Killough, and Koh (2001) considered task complexity when evaluating the relationship between performance and self-efficacy. Mohammed, Mathieu, and Bartlett (2002) included leadership when considering task type. Zigurs and Buckland (1998) used the McGrath (1984) Circumplex and classified tasks as behavior descriptions, ability requirements, task materials, and behavioral requirements. Liu and Li (2012) classified task types according to goals of input and output, process, time, and presentation. Liu and Li also reported that tasks could be measured subjectively and objectively depending on the goal of the task and output. Pieschl (2012) considered Bloom's taxonomy and suggested that task characteristics could be: remember, understand, apply, analyze, and evaluate. Salimi, (2012) also indicated that tasks can be characterized by complexity, condition, difficulty, resources, and participant ability. Technology has also complicated task complexity by solving some problems and creating new ones (Rescher, 1998). Slear, Reames, Susan, Maggard, and Connelly (2016) have done some work related to the impact of technology on tasks by identifying a connection between task clarity, task complexity, and task control in distance education.

Task Complexity

The literature abounds in models and definitions of task complexity. There are three approaches: structural, resource requirements, and interaction (Liu & Li, 2012). The structural approach has been constructed around task structure, the number, and relationship of elements involved in a task. Several researchers (Campbell, 1988; Ham, Park, & Jung, 2012; Liu & Li, 2012; Wood, 1986; Zigurs & Buckland, 1998) have used Bonner (1994) to link task complexity to task structure.

The resource requirement approach (Liu & Li, 2012) views task complexity in terms of resource requirements such as human information processing and cognitive demands. Liu and Li (2012) linked Braarud (2001), Wickens and McCarley (2008), and Park (2009) to this approach. Li and Wieringa (2000) emphasized physical and mental demand requirements, Bettman, Johnson, and Payne (1990) emphasized cognitive efforts, and Jacko, Salvend, and Koubeck (1995) emphasized short-term memory requirements.

Liu and Li (2012) also identified an interaction approach to task complexity. Prior knowledge and experience interact with the task. Complexity is then contingent upon the person doing the task (Gonzalez, Vanyukov, & Martin, 2005). The interaction between the person and the task can involve seeking information, understanding information requirements, uncertainty, and process (Bystrom & Jarvelin, 1995). Other researchers have understood task complexity it terms of the interaction of task components (Funke, 2010).

Task Measures

Once task characteristics have been defined and identified, task complexity can be measured. Mascha and Miller (2010) evaluated tasks using cues to determine if the task can be considered simple or difficult. If information has already been provided, the task can be determined as simple. If information is not provided, the task will be more difficult. Tasks are most often measured by difficulty and ranked from high to low (Bolt et al., 2001; Convertino, 2008; Hackman, 1968; Jacques, Garger, Brown, & Deale, 2009; Mascha & Miller, 2010; Piescahl, 2012).

Online Personality and Teams

Team effectiveness and personality have been linked (Barrick, Stewart, Neubert, & Mount, 1998; Brandstatter & Farhofer, 1997; Driskell, Hogan, & Salas, 1998; Hack-man & Morris, 1975; Moreland & Levine, 1992; de Jong, Bouhuys, & Barnhoorn, 1999; O'Neil & Kline, 2008). Irani, Telg, Scherler, and Harrington (2003), found that individual personality differences may play a role in distance education students' course performance as well as how they perceive their learning experience. Tseng, Ku, Wang, and Sun (2009) suggested that personality recognition is a key factor in online collaboration and teamwork satisfaction.

Insights Discovery (ID)

ID is based on the personality type theory of Jung (1921). Jung suggested that a component of rational personality (cognitive processes) is the result of interaction between two attitudes (extroversion and introversion) and two functions (thinking and feeling). Attitudes are fundamental orientations, which shape the individual's experience and cognitive process. For example, in the extraverted attitude, external factors are the chief motivating force for judgments, perceptions, feelings, and actions. The external world of activities, things, and people are preferred. See Figure 1.

The psychological nature of introversion is the opposite, with a preference of internal or subjective factors. Introverts are characterized by a preferred orientation that highlights the internal world. This world includes thoughts, feelings, fantasies, and dreams (A. Drummond, personal communication, November 23, 2014).

Functions are also fundamental in individual experience and cognitive process. Thinking features the utilization of rational processes to link conceptually elements of both internal and external experience. Thinking is essentially impersonal and is an objective mental process of interpreting perceptions. Its goal is objective truth, independent of the personality and wishes of another person. Thinkers are at their best with the impersonal and they are most able to handle things that need to be done impersonally (A. Drummond,

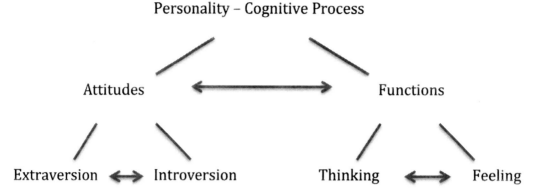

FIGURE 1
Jungian Personality (1921)

personal communication, November 23, 2014).

Feeling, while also a rational cognitive process, is much more personal and occurs on a heart level. Feelers evaluate on the basis of reflection. They use a subjective process that may be independent of external stimuli. As a cognitive process, it often serves as a filter for information that matches what is valued and wanted (A. Drummond, personal communication, November 23, 2014).

These attitudes and functions interact to create "attitudinal functions," and it is these interactions that create personality types (e.g., orientations to extraversion and thinking combine to create the "extraverted thinking" type). These personality types represent differences in cognitive process. ID presents this balance in terms of four colors. The colors are used entirely for ease of use and recall in learning and development environments where people struggle to remember attitudinal functions. The colors are summarized in Figure 2 (Insights, 2014). A sample ID Report can be reviewed at this site: http://hrc.co.in/wp-content/uploads/2013/06/Sample-Insights-Discovery.pdf

ID is widely used in private, nonprofit, and government organizations. ID has offices in 12 African countries, 26 European countries, eight Asian countries, and seven offices in the United States and Canada (https://www.insights.com/us/develop-your-business-using-insights-discovery/). Four million people have used ID, including employees of leading organizations (e.g., Expedia, LinkedIn, Microsoft, Philips, Allergan, AstraZeneca, and Technip) (https://www.insights.com/us/case-studies/).

ID has been registered by the British Psychological Society (BPS) and tested by their testing center (PTC). The British Psychological Society test registration is based on the European Federation of Psychologists Association's Review Model for the Description and Evaluation of tests. A test receives the British Psychological Society Certificate of Test Registration if it meets European Federation of Psychologists' Associations standards for validity, reliability, and norms. The European Federation of Psychologists' Association is used across Europe to support and encourage the harmonizing of European tests (http://ptc.bps.org.uk/test-registration-test-reviews). Test summary reviews are available (http://ptc.bps.org.uk/test-registration-test-reviews). The ID has also been presented at the 11th European Congress of Psychology.

Figure 2 gives an overview of the ID four personality types, and Figures 3 and 4 illustrate the relationship of ID type/color and cognitive process. In Figure 3, the ID attitudes (Extroversion/Introversion) are identified with the ID left/right circle halves, with Blue and Green as

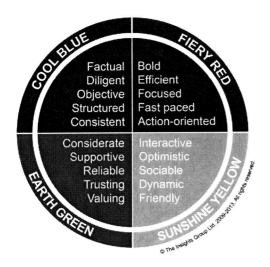

FIGURE 2
ID Four Personality Types

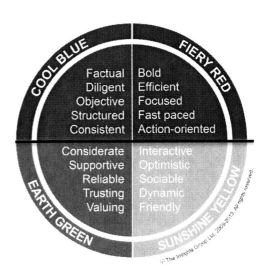

FIGURE 4
Linking ID Function to Cognitive Process
(Thinking/Feeling)

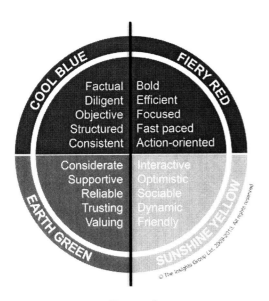

FIGURE 3
Linking ID Attitude to Cognitive Process
(Extroversion/Introversion)

nitive process and Green and Yellow as the feeling cognitive process.

Personality Type Bias and Team Performance on Complex Tasks

Bias can impact team performance (Convertino, 2008). A review of the research indicates that groups that are similar or homogeneous share common beliefs and are therefore more biased, while groups that have a diverse composition are less biased. Groups that are not homogeneous tend to perform at a higher level. However, increased diversity could also reduce team performance if there was insufficient time to build common ground (Convertino, 2008).

This bias could be related to group process (Kerr & Tindale, 2004). Views from the minority are less likely to be considered, even when the view is critical. Gigone and Hastier (1996) referred to this phenomenon as a common knowledge effect. Biases prevent teams from the benefit of different skills and knowledge. When increased diversity leads to increased shared perspective and knowledge,

the introverted cognitive process and Red and Yellow as the extroverted cognitive process. In Figure 4, the ID functions (Thinking/Feeling) are identified with the ID upper/lower circle halves, with Blue and Red as the thinking cog-

teams can improve their performance (van Knippenberg & Schippers, 2007).

RESEARCH METHOD

Hypotheses

H1: Teams dominated by Extroverts (ID Fiery Red and Sunshine Yellow) tend to outperform teams dominated with Introverts (ID Cool Blue and Earth Green) on complex tasks.

H2: Teams dominated by Thinking members (ID Fiery Red and Cool Blue) tend to outperform teams dominated by Feeling members (ID Earth Green and Sunshine Yellow) on complex tasks.

H3: Teams dominated by Fiery Red ID types tend to outperform teams dominated by Sunshine Yellow ID, Earth Green ID, or Cool Blue ID on complex tasks.

H4: Teams with a lower bias (Variable teams with all four ID types) tend to outperform teams with a higher bias (teams with one Dominant ID type) with complex tasks.

Research Approach

The study used a general mixed method linking qualitative and quantitative methods. Each researcher received training in understanding ID. Qualitative data were collected as researchers were paired to assess student ID types and categorized student teams as Dominant or Variable (Table 2). ID types and team categorization did not proceed until there was full consensus. In the event consensus could not be reached, a research group member who was ID certified served as the final arbitrator. Those student teams that did not have a complete clear record of ID types for each student were excluded from the study. Quantitative data were collected from the numerical scores of student team assignments, which were then reviewed descriptively by t tests and ANOVA.

Measuring the Operationalization of Complexity

This study framed task complexity from the Bonner structural perspective. Bonner (1994) utilized a task model involving input, processing, and output. Twenty factors are then included and organized by information and clarity of information for each of the task model components of output, processing, and output (see Figure 5).

The study involved three tasks of varying complexity. In Week 1, each team wrote a 600-word memo describing each member, using their ID type and previous work experience to introduce the team to the class. The memo addressed team challenges and strengths (see Appendix A).

In Week 5, each team completed the course Market Simulation that ran in each of the previous weeks. In addition to completing the last Market Simulation Unit, in Week 5 teams were ranked with a Cumulative Balanced Scorecard based on their team performance, including the Market Simulation variables of total demand, stocks out, emergency loan, bankruptcy, net income, ending cash flow, retained earnings, and balanced scorecard (see Appendix B).

In Week 6, each team prepared a 16-slide PowerPoint presentation. The presentation addressed appropriate next steps for their simulated business at the end of the simulation. The presentation analyzed the previous four quarters (each week was identified as a business quarter) and completed a tactical plan, pro forma financial statements, and business plan through the 6th quarter (see Appendix C).

Based on the Bonner Task Complexity Model, Week 5 (ranked 3) was the most complex, followed by the Week 6 assignment, with the Week 1 assignment (ranked 1) being the least complex (see Table 1).

Task Complexity	Input	Amount	Number of Alternatives Number of Cues Cue Redundancy
		Clarity	Cue Specification Cue Measurement Match Between Presented Cues Presentation Format
	Processing	Amount	Number of Alternatives Number of Cues Number of Procedures
		Clarity	Procedure Specification Procedure Interdependence Sign of Input-Output Relations Magnitude of Input-Output Relations Cue Consistency Functional Form of Process
	Output	Amount	Number of Goals Number of Solutions
		Clarity	Goal Specification Presence of Criteria for Testing Solutions

Source: Bonner (1994).

FIGURE 5
Bonner's Model of Task Complexity

TABLE 1
Assignment Task Complexity Ranking

		Unit 1 Task Memo	*Unit 6 Task PowerPoint (PPT)*	*Unit 5 Task Market Simulation*
Input	Amount	1	2	3
	Clarity	1	2	3
Process	Amount	1	2	3
	Clarity	1	2	3
Output	Amount	1	2	3
	Clarity	1	2	3

Source: Bonner (1994 p. 215).

Measuring the Operationalization of Team Composition in Terms of Personality

Nominal data were utilized to categorize teams. Teams where the majority of team members had one ID type were categorized as Dominant. Those teams where there was at least one team member from each ID type where categorized as Variable. As a result,

Variable teams were the most heterogeneous with the lowest bias (see Table 2).

Sample

The sample for this study consisted of students from the initial course of an MBA program course at a proprietary university. The initial sample included 71 classes and 1,800 student-learning teams. The sample was delimited

TABLE 2
Team Personality Types and Bias Definition

Team Type	Definition	Bias
Dominant	50% of members with the same personality; all other personalities at less than 50%	High
Variable	All personalities were present	Low

Source: Olson et al. (2015).

TABLE 3
Extroversion (Red/Yellow ID) Compared To Introversion (Blue/Green ID) Team Personality by Task

	Task #1 (Memo)		Task #2 (Mkt Sim)		Task #3 (Team PPT)	
	Extra Version	Intro Version	Extra Version	Intro Version	Extra Version	Intro Version
Mean team scores	93.06	92.53	92.55	89.83	91.19	91.71
Variance	38.29	59.92	36.76	27.28	41.94	32.98
Observations	27	57	27	57	27	57
Pooled variance	53.06		30.29		35.82	
df	82		82		82	
$P(T <= t)$ one-tail	0.378		0.019		0.355	

by only including teams that met the following criteria: (a) 4–6 students on the team, (b) all team members completing the course, and (c) all team members providing accurate ID type classification. These delimitations reduced the final sample size to 138 learning teams.

Performance

Faculty grades were used to assess performance. Scores were grouped by assignment based on the level of task complexity and compared for difference by personality type. Dominant and variable team performance was compared by assignment task complexity.

RESULTS

Hypothesis 1

H1: Teams dominated by Extroverts (ID Fiery Red and Sunshine Yellow) tend to outperform teams dominated with Intro-

verts (ID Cool Blue and Earth Green) on complex tasks.

As shown in Table 3, the "t Test: Two Sample Assuming Equal Variance" procedure was used to evaluate hypothesis 1. No statistically significant difference was found in comparing team scores for tasks #1 (Team Memo) and #3 (Team Presentation). However, a statistically significant difference was found in comparing team scores for task #2 (Market Simulation) at a 95% confidence level. Teams where the majority of members had an Attitude of Extroversion outperformed teams where the majority of members had an Attitude of Introversion. Hypothesis $H1_0$ is not supported for the less complex Tasks #1 and #3, but is supported for the more complex Task #2 at the 95% confidence level.

Hypothesis 2

H2: Teams dominated by Thinking members (ID Fiery Red and Cool Blue) tend

TABLE 4
Thinking (Red/Blue ID) Compared To Feeling (Green/Yellow ID) Team, Personality by Task

	Task #1 (Memo)		Task #2 (Mkt Sim)		Task #3 (Team PPT)	
	Thinking	*Feeling*	*Thinking*	*Feeling*	*Thinking*	*Feeling*
Mean team scores	92.72	92.66	90.63	90.88	91.71	91.15
Variance	48.89	63.35	32.80	29.82	32.88	42.92
Observations	59	25	59	25	59	25
Pooled variance	53.125		31.930		35.817	
df	82		82		82	
$P(T <= t)$ one-tail	0.486		0.426		0.347	
$P(T <= t)$ two-tail	0.972		0.853		0.693	

to outperform teams dominated by Feeling members (ID Earth Green and Sunshine Yellow) on complex tasks.

The "*t* Test: Two Sample Assuming Equal Variance" procedure was again used to evaluate hypotheses $H2_0$. Table 4 shows that no statistically significant difference was found in comparing each set of task scores. Hypothesis $H2_0$ is not supported for any of the three tasks.

Hypothesis 3

H3: Teams dominated by Fiery Red ID types tend to outperform teams dominated by Sunshine Yellow ID, Earth Green ID, or Cool Blue ID on complex tasks.

To assess $H3_0$, a one-way analysis of variance (ANOVA) procedure was applied to each set of task scores. There was no statistically significant difference between any of the personality styles for any of the tasks (see Tables 5a, 5b, 5c, and the summary in Table 5d). Hypothesis $H3_0$ is not supported for any of the three tasks.

Hypothesis 4

H4: Teams with a lower bias (Variable teams with all four ID types) tend to out-

perform teams with a higher bias (teams with one Dominant ID type) with complex tasks.

The "*t* Test: Two Sample Assuming Equal Variance" procedure was also used to evaluate hypotheses $H4_0$. Table 6 shows that no statistically significant difference was found in comparing each set of task scores at the two-tail p-value level. There was no statistically significant difference in team performance between teams with lower bias (teams with all four personality type) and teams with higher bias (teams with one dominant personality type).

However, teams with higher bias (teams with one dominant personality type) outperformed teams with lower bias (teams with all four personality types) on Task #2 (Market Simulation) using a one-tail p value ($p = 0.037$). Hypothesis $H4_0$ is not supported for Tasks #1 and #3, but it is supported for Task #2 using a one-tail test of significance.

DISCUSSION

A previous study by this group examined the relationship between virtual team performance and ID personality type. The findings did not indicate a relationship between virtual team performance and ID personality type (Olsen et al., 2015). There was no statistically significant difference in the performance of any per-

TABLE 5A
ANOVA: Comparison of Personality Type Using Task #1 (Team Memo) Scores

Personality Type	Count	Sum	Mean Team Scores	Variance
Red	20	1,853.58	92.67	38.269
Blue	39	3,616.85	92.73	55.488
Green	18	1,657.38	92.07	73.042
Yellow	7	659.08	94.15	42.834

Team Performance	Sum of Squares	df	Mean Square	F	Significance
Between groups	21.867	3	7.289	0.135	0.939
Within groups	4,334.409	80	54.180		

TABLE 5B
ANOVA: Comparison of Personality Type Using Task #2 (Market Simulation) Scores

Personality Type	Count	Sum	Mean Team Scores	Variance
Red	20	1,862.93	93.15	39.326
Blue	39	3,484.11	89.36	25.351
Green	18	1,636.03	90.89	31.448
Yellow	7	635.944	90.85	30.184

Team Performance	Sum of Squares	df	Mean Square	F	Significance
Between groups	193.086	3	64.363	2.122	0.104
Within groups	2,426.270	80	30.328		

TABLE 5C
ANOVA: Comparison of Personality Type Using Task #3 (Team PowerPoint) Scores

Personality Type	Count	Sum	Mean Team Scores	Variance
Red	20	1,854.30	92.71	31.994
Blue	39	3,556.65	91.19	33.384
Green	18	1,670.84	92.82	32.111
Yellow	7	607.805	86.82	50.490

Team Performance	Sum of Squares	df	Mean Square	F	Significance
Between groups	217.276	3	72.425	2.126	0.103
Within groups	2,725.313	80	34.066		

sonality ID type, or grouping of ID personality types on virtual team performance. Further, there was no statistically significant difference based on ID personality type bias. That is, heterogeneous teams and homogenous teams demonstrated no significant difference in team performance. However, while completing this study, the research group did notice differences in ID personality type team performance related to task complexity. This study was

TABLE 5D
Summary of ANOVA on Team Scores for Task Type

Team Performance	Sum of Squares	df	Mean Square	F	Significance
Task #1 (Memo)					
Between Groups	21.867	3	7.289	0.135	0.939
Within Groups	4,334.409	80	54.180		
Task #2 (Market Simulation)					
Between Groups	193.086	3	64.363	2.122	0.104
Within Groups	2,426.270	80	30.328		
Task #3 (Team PowerPoint)					
Between Groups	217.276	3	72.425	2.126	0.103
Within Groups	2,725.313	80	34.066		

TABLE 6
Lower Bias Compared to Higher Bias Team Personality by Task

	Task #1 (Memo)		Task #2 (Mkt Sim)		Task #3 (Team PPT)	
	Lower Bias	Higher Bias	Lower Bias	Higher Bias	Lower Bias	Higher Bias
Mean team scores	90.90	92.70	88.03	90.70	90.80	91.54
Variance	32.01	52.49	53.91	31.56	59.85	35.45
Observations	20	84	20	84	20	84
Pooled variance	48.671		35.723		39.997	
df	102		102		102	
$P(T <= t)$ one-tail	0.151		0.037		0.318	
$P(T <= t)$ two-tail	0.301		0.075		0.636	

completed to investigate the relationship of task complexity, ID personality type, attitudinal preferences of extroversion/introversion and functional preferences of thinking/feeling to virtual team performance.

These subsequent findings suggest that personality types with the attitude of extroversion will do better on complex tasks than personality types with the attitude of introversion. Biased teams (teams with 50% or more of the team consisting of one personality type) also were more effective with complex tasks than unbiased teams. However, personality types with the function of thinking or feeling showed no performance difference related to task complexity and there was no variation in the performance of complex tasks related to any one

personality type. Each personality type did equally as well with complex tasks.

One would expect that the lean virtual environment would favor teams with the attitude of introversion, given the restrictions of the communication medium for extroverted interaction; however, the study indicated that teams with the attitude of extroversion did better with complex tasks than teams with the attitude of introversion. Perhaps the extroverted team members mitigated the increased potential for withdrawal in a virtual environment with their preference for the external world of things, people, and activities. Extroverts worked against the potential isolation of virtual communication mediums, which increased their performance compared to introverted teams that may have followed the isolating flow of the communication medium. Teams with a dominance of introverted team members were reinforced in their preferences for the internal world by communication mediums that supported that preference and may have avoided interaction, the result being reduced interaction and diminished performance on complex tasks. Workman, Kahnweiler, and Bommer, (2003) did observe that team members preferring group interaction demonstrated more commitment to virtual teamwork.

One would also expect unbiased teams would perform better on complex tasks than biased teams, given the additional perspective and processing; however, this was not substantiated by the study. Time pressure could have been a mitigating factor. Each team had one week to complete each assignment. Teams with a similar personality type and approach in its attitudes and functions could be more time-efficient, resulting in better performance with complex tasks. Unbiased teams may not have had sufficient time to take advantage of their diversity.

Task complexity may open new windows of understanding related to the impact of personality on performance. Some researchers have suggested that personality could be demonstrated to be a factor in virtual team performance (Barrick et al., 1998; Brandstatter & Farhofer, 1997; de Jong et al., 1999; Hackman & Morris, 1975; Moreland & Levine, 1992; O'Neil & Kline, 2008), while other researchers have suggested that there is no correlation between team effectiveness and personality (Beise et al., 2010; Chantal et al., 2010; Faizuniah & Chan, 2014; Hackman & Morris, 1975; Moreland & Levine, 1992; Rutti et al., 2012). Like these researchers, our initial study did not suggest a relationship between personality type and performance; however, the subsequent study did suggest a relationship between task complexity and personality. The frame of task complexity may explain these varying results related to personality and team performance.

Some researchers have reported no clear relationship between the attitudes of extroversion and functions of thinking/feeling and team performance (Kim, Lee, Lee, Huang, & Makany, 2011; Liu & Li, 2012). Like Hayes and Allison (1998), this study pointed toward a relationship of attitudes and functions with team performance. While this study did not indicate a relationship between the functions of thinking/feeling with team performance, there was some performance difference on complex tasks related to the attitudes of extroversion/introversion. Hayes and Allison (1998) linked the functions of thinking/feeling to differentiation of global and local thinking. Individuals using local functions prefer data (facts), while individuals using global functions prefer using knowledge (meaning). This study did indicate a difference between attitudes and functions related to the performance of complex tasks; however, the difference was not with the functions of thinking/feeling. The difference was with the attitudes of extroversion/introversion.

Our previous study did not find any performance difference between biased and unbiased groups (reference redacted for peer review), which did not support Convertino's (2008) findings suggesting a relationship between bias (diversity of personality type) and virtual team performance. This study did indicate a correlation based on task complexity between personality type, team bias, and performance; however, the findings did not support Convertino's (2008) findings. Instead of bias (homogeneity) leading to decreased performance, in this study bias led to increased performance on complex tasks. While bias did affect the performance of complex tasks, it was the high-bias homogenous teams that outperformed the low-bias heterogeneous teams on complex tasks. Diversity appeared to be a detriment. The study did not assess the decision-making of homogeneous groups (Gigone & Hastier, 1996; Tolcott, Marvin, & Lehner, 1989; van Knippenberg & Schippers, 2007) or the bias of group processing in homogeneous groups (Kerr & Tindale, 2004), the study could only report that increased bias led to increased performance with complex tasks.

RECOMMENDATIONS

So how should professors assign teams to position them for success? This study would suggest that time pressure and task complexity drive team assignments. When teams have very short time horizons, biased teams would likely outperform unbiased teams. With complex tasks, teams with a dominance of extroverted members would likely outperform teams with a dominance of introverted members. While ID personality type is a factor in team performance, it needs to be intentionally linked to task complexity and time pressure. The leading independent variables are bias and the attitude of extroversion/introversion. ID personality type does not appear to be a factor.

In online environments, by observing student behavior through introduction and discussion board threads, professors could make some assessments related to student attitude (extroverted/introverted), function (thinking/feeling), and ID personality type. When making team assignments, those assessments could then be paired with task complexity and time pressure to position teams for success. Wade, Cameron, Morgan, and Williams (2016) conclude that understanding how to best work with others toward a common goal and how to structure group work in online educational settings are critical components in developing students who are competitive in today's workplace market.

LIMITATIONS

The study may have been improved if either the resource or interaction approach to task complexity had been used instead of the structural approach used in the study. This study used a structural frame to assess task complexity with an emphasis on the task itself, and the number and kind of elements involved in a task (Bonner, 1994; Campbell, 1988; Ham et al.,

2012; Wood, 1986; Zigurs & Buckland, 1998). The resource and interaction approach may have given more pronounced differences with the performance of complex tasks given their emphasis on the human resource requirements and processes for a task.

The resource approach categorizes task complexity by the human resources needed to complete the task, human resources such as information processing and cognitive processes. The interaction approach also centers on the person doing the task, but the emphasis is on interaction instead of human resources (Braarud, 2001; Bettman et al, 1990; Jacko et al., 1995; Li & Wieringa, 2000; Park, 2009; Wickens & McCarley, 2008). The interaction approach does not focus on the human resource requirements related to experience, knowledge, and training, but focuses on human resource requirements related to interaction. Not what is known, but how knowledge emerges through interaction (Bystrom & Jarvelin, 1995; Gonzales et al., 2005). Both the resource and interaction approaches to task complexity would link more closely to the independent variable of personality type with its attitudes of extroversion/introversion and functions of thinking/feeling than the structure approach used in the study.

As always, improved sampling would have been beneficial. While the sample was taken over a 2-year period, the sample was taken from one course early in an online propriety MBA program. A strengthened sample would have included a class toward the end of the MBA program. Technology adaptation is a factor that should be considered in an early online course that could be mitigated with a course added to the sample toward the end of the MBA.

Although the ID describes 64 personality types, this study was limited to the four that subjects self-disclosed in a team assignment used in the study. The full strength of the ID was not put into play, which may have yielded more granular findings. Using only four of the 64 types may have masked differences between personality types.

Grade inflation may have also been a limitation and should be addressed in subsequent similar studies. The initial study did not indicate performance difference, partly because so many students were given an A. There was not sufficient grade variation to indicate difference. This study did find difference in the context of grade inflation on the criteria of task complexity. While this did have value, grade inflation may have hidden more significant differences.

Time pressure is also a variable of importance that should be included in subsequent studies. ID types, their attitudes, functions and degree of bias could perform differently based on time pressure. Bias simplifies team processes, which would be beneficial in time urgent situations. Unbiased teams will likely require more time to capitalize on the additional perspectives and approaches represented by different ID types, attitudes, and functions. This would have value to help online groups develop the time management skills required for professional workforce settings (Morgan, Williams, Cameron, & Wade, 2014).

REFERENCES

Barrick, M. R., Stewart, G. L., Neubert, M. J., & Mount, M. K. (1998). Relating member ability and personality to work-team processes and team effectiveness. *Journal of Applied Psychology, 83,* 43–51.

Barry, B., & Stewart, G. L. (1997). Composition, process, and performance in self-managed groups: The role of personality. *Journal of Applied Psychology, 82,* 62–78.

Beise, C., Carte, T., Vician, C., & Chidambaram, L. (2010). A case study of project management practices in virtual settings: Lessons from working in and managing virtual teams. *Database for Advances in Information Systems, 41*(4), 75–97.

Bettman, J. R., Johnson, E. J., & Payne, J. W. (1990). A componential analysis of cognitive effort in choice. *Organizational Behavior and Human Decision Processes, 45*(1), 111–139.

Bolt, A., M., Killough, M. L. N., & Koh, H. C. (2001). Testing the interaction effects of task complexity in computer training using the social

cognitive model. *Decision Sciences, 32*(1), 1–20.

Bonner, S. E. (1994). A model of the effects of audit task complexity. *Accounting, Organizations and Society, 19*(3), 213–234.

Braarud, P. O. (2001). Subjective task complexity and subjective workload: criterion validity for complex team tasks. *International Journal of Cognitive Ergonomics, 5*(3), 261–273.

Brandstatter, H., & Farthofer, A. (1997). Personality in social influence across tasks and groups. *Small Group Research, 28,* 146–163.

Bystrom, K., & Javelin, K. (1995). Task complexity affects information seeking and use. *Information Processing and Management, 31*(2), 191–213.

Campbell, D., J. (1988). Task complexity: a review and analysis. *The Academy of Management Review, 13*(1), 40–52.

Carver, D. L., Kosloski, M. F., Jr. (2015). Analysis of student perceptions of the psychosocial learning environment in online and face-to-face career and technical education courses. *Quarterly Review of Distance Education, 16*(4), 7–22.

Chantel, M. J. H., Beatrice, I. J. M., & Peoll, R. F. (2010). Attitudes towards factors influencing team performance: A multi-rater approach aimed at establishing the relative importance of team learning behaviors in comparison with other predictors of team performance. *Team Performance Management, 16*(7/8), 451–474.

Convertino, M. P. (2008). The CACHE Study: *Group Effects in Computer Supported Cooperative Work, 17*(10), 353–393.

de Jong, R. D., Bouhuys, S. A., & Barnhoorn, J. C. (1999). Personality, self-efficacy and functioning in management teams: A contribution to validation. *International Journal of Selection and Assessment, 7,* 46–49.

Driskell, J. E., Hogan, R., & Salas, E. (1998). Personality and group performance. *Review of Personality and Social Psychology, 14,* 91–112.

Faizuniah P., & Chan, J. M. (2014). The mediating effect of knowledge sharing on the relationship between trust and virtual team effectiveness. *Journal of Knowledge Management, 18*(1), 92–106.

Funke, J. (2010). Complex problem solving: A case for complex cognition? *Cognitive Processing, 11*(2), 133–142.

Gigone, D., & Hastier, R. (1996). The impact of information on small group choice. *Journal of Personality and Social Psychology, 72,* 132–140. doi: 10.1037/0022-3514.72.1.132.

Gonzalez, C., Vanyukov, P., & Martin, M. K. (2005). The use of microworlds to study dynamic decision making. *Computers in Human Behavior, 12*(2), 273–286.

Goold, A., Craig, A., & Coldwell, J. (2008). *The student experience of working in teams online.* Paper presented at the Ascilite Melbourne Conference. Retrieved from http://www.ascilite .org.au/conferences/melbourne08/procs/goold .pdf

Hackman, J. R. (1968). Effects of task characteristics on group products. *Journal of Experimental Social Psychology, 4,* 162–187.

Hackman, J. R., 1969. Toward understanding the role of tasks in behavior research. *Acta Psychologica, 31,* 97–128.

Hackman, J. R., & Morris, C. G. (1975). Group tasks, group interaction process, and group performance effectiveness: A review and proposed integration. *Advances in Experimental Social Psychology, 8,* 45–99.

Hackman, J. R., & Oldham, G. R. (1976) Motivation through the design of work: Test of a theory. *Organizational Behavior and Human Performance, 16*(2), 250–279.

Ham, D. H., Park, J.,& Jung, W. (2012). Model-based identification and use of task complexity factors of human integrated systems. *Reliability Engineering & System Safety, 100,* 33–47.

Hayes, J., & Allison, C.W. (1998). Cognitive style and theory and practice of individual and collective learning in organizations. *Human Relations, 51*(7), 847–871

Hewson, L., & Hughes, C. (2005). Social processes and pedagogy in online learning. *Association for the Advancement of Computing in Education Journal, 13*(2), 99–125.

Irani, T., Telg, R., Scherler, C., & Harrington, M. (2003). Personality type and its relationship to distance education students' course perceptions and performance. *Quarterly Review of Distance Education, 4*(4), 445–453.

Jacko, J. A., Salvendy, G., & Koubeck, R. J. (1995). Modeling of menu design in computerized work. *Interacting with Computers, 7*(3), 304–330.

Jacques, G. B., Garger, J., Brown, C. A., & Deale, C. S. (2009). Personality and virtual reality team candidates: The roles of personality traits, technology anxiety and trust as predicators of perceptions of virtual reality teams. *Journal of Business Management, 15*(2), 146–157.

Jung, C. G. (1971). Psychological types. In *The collected works of C. G. Jung* (Vol. 60). Princeton, NJ: Princeton University Press.

Kerr, N. L., & Tindale, S. R. (2004). Group performance and decision-making. *Annual Review of Psychology, 55,* 623–665. doi:10.1146/annureve .pscyh.55.090902.142099

Kim, P., Lee, D., Lee, Y., Huang, C., & Makany, T. (2011). *Team Performance Management, 17*(1/2), 41–62.

Kline, T. J. B. (1999). *Remaking teams: The revolutionary research based guide that puts theory into practice.* San Francisco, CA: Jossey-Bass.

Kline, T., & O'Grady, J. K. (2009). Team member personality, team processes, and outcomes: Relationships within a graduate student project team sample. *North American Journal of Psychology, 11*(2), 369–382.

Li, K., & Wieringa, P. A. (2000). Understanding perceived complexity in human supervisory control. *Cognition, Technology and Work, 2*(2), 75–88.

Liu, P. L., & Li, Z. (2012). Task complexity: A review and conceptualization framework. *International Journal of Industrial Ergonomics, 42*(2012), 553–568.

MacDonnell, R., O'Neill, T., Kline, T., & Hambley, L. (2009). Bringing group-level personality to the electronic realm: A comparison of face-to-face and virtual contexts. *The Psychologist-Manager Journal, 12.* doi:10.1080/10887150802371773

Mascha, M. F., & Miller, C. (2010). The effects of task complexity and skill on over/under-estimation of internal control. *Managerial Auditing Journal, 25*(8), 734–755.

McGrath, J. E. (1984). *Groups: Interaction and performance.* Englewood Cliffs, NJ: Prentice-Hall.

McInnerney, J. M., & Roberts, T. S. (2004). Online learning: Social interaction and the creation of a sense of community. *Educational Technology & Society, 7*(3), 73–81.

Mohammed, S., Mathieu, J. E., & Bartlett, A. L. (2002). Technical-administrative task performance, leadership task performance, and contextual performance: Considering the influence of team and task related composition variables. *Journal of Organizational Behavior, 23*(7), 795–814.

Moreland, R. L., & Levine, J. M. (1992). *Problem identification by groups.* In S. Worshel, W. Wood, & J. A. Simpson (Eds.), *Group process and productivity* (pp. 17–47). New York, NY: SAGE.

Morgan, K., Williams, K. C., Cameron, B. A., Wade, C. E. (2014). Faculty perceptions of online group work. *Quarterly Review of Distance Education, 15*(4), 37-42.

Olson, J., Ringhand, D., Kalinsky, R., & Ziegler, J. (2015). Forming student online teams for maximum performance. *American Journal of Business Education, 8*(2). 139–160. doi:http://dx.doi.org/10.19030/ajbe.v8i2.9136

O'Neill, T., & Kline, T. (2008). Personality as a predictor of teamwork: A business simulator study. *North American Journal of Psychology, 10*(1), 65-78.

Palloff, R. M., & Pratt, K. (1999). *Building learning communities in cyberspace: Effective strategies for the online classroom.* San Francisco, CA: Jossey-Bass.

Park, J. (2009). *The complexity of proceduralized tasks.* London, England: Springer.

Pieschl, S. S. (2012). Is adaptation to task complexity really beneficial for performance? *Learning and Instruction, 22,* 281-289.

Potter, R. E., & Balthazard, P. A. (2002). Understanding human interaction and performance in the virtual team. *Journal of Information Technology Theory and Application, 4,* 1–23.

Rescher, N. (1998). *Complexity: A philosophical overview.* Brunswick, NJ: Transaction.

Rutti, R., Ramsey, I. R., & Li, C. (2012). The role of other orientation in team selection and anticipated performance. *Team Performance Management, 18*(1/2), 41–58.

Salimi, A. D. (2012). Task complexity and SL development: Does task complexity matter? *ScienceDirect, 46,* 726–735.

Seung, W. Y. (2006). Two group development patterns of virtual learning teams. *Quarterly Review of Distance Education, 7*(3), 297–312.

Slear, J. N., Reames, E. H., Susan, E., Maggard, P., & Connelly, D. A. (2016). Creating equivalent learning outcomes in a distance education leadership course. *Quarterly Review of Distance Education, 17*(2), 1–14.

Straus, S. G. (1996). Getting a clue: The effects of communication media and information distribution on participation and performance in computer-mediated and face-to-face groups. *Small Group Research, 27,* 115–142.

Taggar, S. (2000). *Personality, cognitive ability, and behavior: The antecedents of effective autonomous work teams.* Dissertation Abstracts International, 60(9–A).

Tolcott, M. A., Marvin, F. F., & Lehner, P. E. (1989). Expert decision making in evolving situations. *IEEE Transactions on Systems, Man, and Cybernetics, 19*(3), 606–615. doi:10.1109/21.31066

Topi, H., Valacich, J. S., & Rao, M. T. (2002). The effects of personality and media differences on the performance of dyads addressing a cognitive conflict task. *Small Group Research, 33,* 667–701.

Tseng, H., Ku, H.-Y., Wang, C.-H., & Sun, L. (2009). Key factors in online collaboration and their relationship to teamwork satisfaction. *Quarterly Review of Distance Education, 10*(2), 195–206.

van Knippenberg, D., & Schippers, M. C. (2007). Work group diversity. *Annual review of Psychology, 58,* 515–545. doi:10.1146/annureve.psych.58.110405.085546

van Vianen, A., & de Dreu, C. (2001). Personality in teams: Its relationship to social cohesion, task cohesion, and team performance. *European Journal of Work and Organizational Psychology, 10,* 97–120.

Wade, C. E., Cameron, B. A., Morgan, K., & Williams, K. C. (2016). Key components of online group projects. *Quarterly Review of Distance Education, 17*(1), 33–42.

Wickens, C. D., & McCarley, J. (2008). *Applied attention theory.* Boca Raton, FL: Taylor & Francis.

Williams, E. A., & Castro, S. L. (2010). The effects of teamwork on individual learning and perceptions of team performance: A comparison of face-to-face and online project settings. *Team Performance Management, 16*(3/4), 124–147.

Wood, R. E. (1986). Task complexity: Definition of the construct. *Organizational Behavior and Human Decision Processes, 37*(1), 60–82.

Workman, M. D., Kahnweiler, W., & Bommer, W. (2003). The effects of cognitive style and media on commitment to telework and virtual teams. *Journal of Vocational Behavior, 63,* 199–219.

Yeatts, D. E., & Hyten, C. (1998). *High-performing self-managed work teams: A comparison of theory to practice.* Thousand Oaks, CA: SAGE.

Zigurs, I., & Buckland, B. K., (1998). A theory of task/technology fit and group support systems effectiveness. *MIS Quarterly, 223,* 313–334.

APPENDIX A

Week 1: Team Memo Assignment

Taken directly from the proprietary online MBA course used in the study.

Team Memo for 30 points

Use your Team Discussion Board to introduce each team member and to exchange information about particular strengths, fields of study, and work experience. Your Team Discussion Board can be accessed from the Team Area Unit (below Unit 6).

Your team should then collaboratively pull this information together into a memo addressed to the instructor and the class (approximately 500–600 words), introducing your team and reviewing your team strengths and challenges. Include an assessment of your team style using Insights information. Post the memo to the main threaded discussion titled Team Memo Discussion.

Use this area to post the completed memo with all of your team information. Make sure to include team introductions, team strengths and challenges, and an assessment of your team style by using the Insights information.

To the left is an image of an Insights Wheel. You may find the Insights Wheel helpful for creating effective teams throughout your graduate program. Click here for a downloadable copy of the Insights Wheel.

Team assignment information is available on the Main Threaded Discussion in Unit 2 labeled Team Discussion, and your team has a private Team Threaded Discussion area under Team Area. You will use this team throughout the course and this private area for other collaborations.

Make sure to post the completed memo to the Unit 2 Team Discussion Thread by Sunday evening.

Team Tools:

- Your team also has a team-specific area in Doc Sharing, an email group list, and a private synchronous chat area, if you choose to use them.
- Teams sometimes use an instant-messaging service, such as AIM or chat.
- Part of your simulation grade is based on team participation. Setting up a specific time each week to check in may be helpful.

The final grade was determined by how well the Team Memo met the grading criteria and individual participation in the team assignment based on Team DB posts.

APPENDIX B

Week 5

Taken directly from the proprietary online MBA course used in the study. The Marketplace Simulation used in the course is from Marketplace Live, http://www.marketplace-simulation.com/. The following Marketplace Simulation Student Instructions and Executive briefings are taken from the course and provided by Marketplace Live.

The Week 5 Team Project is the completion of a Market Simulation that runs throughout the term. The Simulation has 4 quarters. The team's final performance at the end of Week 5 in the fourth quarter determines the team score for this assignment. Each individual's Week 5 Team Project score is based on peer evaluations and the team's success in the business simulation. At the end of simulation there is a "Cumulative Balanced Scorecard" for each team based on their simulation performance (Total Demand, Stock Outs, Emergency Loan, Bankruptcy, Net Income, Ending Cash Flow, Retained Earnings, Balanced Scorecard). Points for the team project are awarded by ranked finish. The team with the highest Cumulative Balanced Scorecard is awarded 75 points, second 68, third, 64, and fourth 60. 75 points are also awarded for involvement based on peer reviews and time logged into the simulation. A perfect score would be 150 points.

What follows are the student directions. The Executive Briefings are the directions that the faculty member provides for each learner group at the start of the quarter.

Marketplace Simulation Student Instructions

Student sign up:

What you need: The Game ID and your "team" number from your professor. You are a team of one for this simulation. You will have an Advisory Board to work with. You will receive your student license number prior to beginning your Unit 2 assignments. The license number will be emailed to your student.kaplan.edu email address.

Executive Briefings With Students

In ground-based simulations, faculty meets with each student for a reflective briefing. It is important to incorporate this personal touch into our simulation experience. This personal touch is very rewarding. It is nice to see the students develop. You start to take a personal interest in each student, and the students love it.

Executive Briefing for Quarter 1

This is a very interesting quarter for the students. They have almost 2,000,000 in their pockets and a sense that anything is possible. And, they are right. However, they have to start making choices that will affect them for the rest of the exercise.

The most important decision the students have to make in Quarter 1 is their initial strategic direction. They will have several opportunities to change this direction, but there is a tendency to stay with their first strategy throughout the game.

There are many strategies that the students can formulate. Fortunately, most of them can be successful if pursued smartly and aggressively. Thus, the big worry is not which of the

many directions to take, but the rationale for taking any direction. Have the students thought through their options and considered the major implications and tradeoffs of each choice? Do they have a vision for how their firm will successfully compete in the marketplace? Most of the major strategic choices are highlighted in the strategic direction area within the software.

During your Quarter 1 executive briefing, probe to make sure the students have considered the following factors in their decision:

1. Size of market for each market segment. Workhorse segment is the largest in terms of numbers. The Mercedes segment looks like a good size segment but this is deceiving because it is very difficult to satisfy their needs until the firm can offer several new R&D features in Quarter 5. The Traveler segment is moderate in size.

2. Profit potential of each market. Workhorse segment offers the greatest profit potential because it will typically result in large production runs, which drive down production cost, thus improving gross margins. The Mercedes would appear to have attractive profit margins, but the sales volumes are fairly small in the early quarters, thus production costs are very high. The Mercedes segment will not be profitable until new R&D goes on the market in Quarter 5 or later. The Traveler segment is also volume sensitive, but not as bad as Mercedes. This segment should be paired with a large volume segment in order to drive down production costs, thus improving gross margins.

3. Size of geographic markets. The largest markets will generate the largest amount of demand, all other things being equal.

4. Propensity of competitors to enter the market. The largest geographic markets and the Workhorse segment will attract the largest number of competitors. Since this is not hard for the students to forecast, some teams will avoid these markets. You might point out to these teams

that competition is not always bad. Each additional competitor brings more attention to the product category and can actually improve overall demand. To be the only competitor in a geographic market or segment, can be bad news. There is a threshold of marketing that must be done to generate interest in the product. One competitor may not be able to stimulate the market sufficiently to make a good profit.

5. Cost to enter the market. The biggest geographic markets will cost the most to enter, but they have the biggest market demand. The small markets might be cheap, but they may not bring in enough demand to drive production costs down to the point that it is profitable. Small markets can be profitable if added to large markets. The large markets are needed to bring production costs down.

6. Cost to compete. The high-end of the market (Mercedes and Travelers) are expensive to serve. They require more expensive components and R&D. The market will favor teams that can deliver superior performance. It will be unmerciful to those that try to get by with minimum technology.

Executive Briefing for Quarter 2

This will be the toughest quarter for the students. They have to make a lot of difficult decisions with very little information. The anxiety level should be at its peak. You need to be encouraging, cautious and demanding. Encourage the students to try different ideas, to experiment with different advertisements, prices, manufacturing settings. They can learn a great deal from the market.

Encourage the students to be cautious. The students should use Quarter 2 to learn what the market wants and then use this knowledge in Quarter 3 to more aggressively pursue their objectives. They should walk before they try to run. They will be much smarter in Quarter 3 than they are in Quarter 2. They will learn what

customers really like and do not like. They will learn how to run a factory, how to coordinate a broad set of marketing tactics and how to project cash flows. They will discover what their competition is trying to do and be able to take advantage of their weaknesses and defend against their strengths.

Executive Briefing for Quarter 3

The focus this quarter is on skillful adjustment. Each team needs to carefully study the available data, determine what needs fixing and what has gone well for the firm. Spend time on the problem areas. Make sure they understand the cause of the problem and the options for improving the situation. They can learn a great deal from the market data. They should not hesitate to copy a good idea.

This quarter might require some morale building. Firms with sizeable emergency loans (over 500,000) and large negative losses (over 800,000 minus) might be down in the spirits. They need to be pumped up, not artificially but through better decisions. Help them see how they can improve. If they know exactly what the problem was (i.e., low brand judgment, few sales people, etc.), their demand and fortunes should improve.

Executive Briefing for Quarter 4

Activities and Guidelines on How to Review Tactical Plans and Pro Forma Statements for the Business Plan

Quarter 4 is the most difficult decision period for the teams. The teams must analyze the results of Quarter 3, make Quarter 4 decisions and prepare a detailed business plan. For this reason, the students should be given 2 weeks to complete Quarter 4 and prepare and present their business plan. They should have one week for Q4 and one week for the business plan.

Here is a suggested sequence of activities for Quarter 4 and the Business Plan.

1. The teams should analyze Quarter 3 results and complete Quarter 4 in the normal manner.
2. The teams should meet with you as the teams would normally regard Quarter 4 and their analysis and decisions.
3. Within a couple of days of completing Quarter 4, the teams should complete the tactical plan and pro forma financial statements through Quarter 6 and submit these to you for review. The tactical plan and pro formas can be reviewed within the team's software or on paper.
4. You should provide feedback on the quality of the planned tactics and pro forma projections. The revised tactical plan and the pro forma financial statements should be turned in with the business plan.
5. The teams should prepare the final Power Point presentation and submit it to you for review a couple of days before the final presentation.
6. You should provide feedback on the quality of the Power Point presentation.
7. The teams should practice the presentation and question and answer secession.
8. Each team is given 15 to 20 minutes to present and up to 20 minutes for Q and A.
9. Everyone on the team must participate in the presentation.

Executive Briefings for Quarter 5

Quarter 5 is a relatively quiet quarter for most teams. They have a plan and they are executing it. Most will feel good about the future and are feeling good about having worked through and presented a rather difficult business plan. Thus, there tends to be few serious problems at this time. They will show up in Quarter 6.

Expect one in eight firms to go bankrupt in Quarter 5. One in three will have emergency loans. Here are a few things to watch for that may cause emergency loans and bankruptcies in Quarter 6.

First, teams that have not done any R&D will face competitors with better brands.

Unless they are competing on price with many distribution outlets, they will lose market share and will probably not make their forecasted numbers.

If a tam has no R&D in progress, I strongly suggest that they begin an R&D program or find someone from whom they can license technology for Quarter 6. Licensing is especially attractive for a team that is low on equity.

Second, there are aggressive teams out there developing their sales outlets. Very conservative teams will be surprised by the jump in demand for some of their competitors. Unless a firm is expanding sales outlets, it is falling behind the competition. You might push them on this point.

Third, the students will be introducing new brands into the market with new technology. There will be a tendency to drop the older brands in favor of the new ones. There is an opportunity here to use the older brands and compete on price and use the new brands to compete on value, at a higher price. If they only have high-priced brands, they will strangle their demand because their price image could be too high for the market. They need some balance. And, if they discontinue advertising for these older brands, they can save money and add to the margin or the ability to drop price. Effectively, they can take advantage of the loyalty built up over the prior quarters.

I like to advise teams to offer multiple brands to each segment. It is a good idea to have a good, better and best brand.

Quarter 6 Executive Briefing—Helping Weak Teams

Quarter 5 can be disastrous. One out of eight teams will have gone bankrupt in Quarter 5 and one in three may have emergency loans.

I would not worry too much about emergency loans. Most teams will recover from this minor setback. Bankruptcy is more serious.

Bankruptcy can occur among good teams because they have overspent on R&D, new sales outlets and new factory capacity. However, these teams will most likely pull out of bankruptcy. Most of what they have done will create more demand which will drive down production costs and improve gross and net margins. As long as they do not become too timid in Quarter 6, they will do fine.

In the case of weak teams, they are typically surprised by the strong teams that have introduced brands with better R&D features, more advertising and more sales outlets. When strong competition is combined with a weak market, revenues will be down which will send profit margins deep into the red.

APPENDIX C

Week 6

Taken directly from the proprietary online MBA course used in the study.

Your final project involves preparing a Team PowerPoint presentation using your Simulation organization and focusing on where to go next with your organization at the end of Quarter 4 for 120 points. Points were allocated for the PPT, peer evaluations, plus engagement based on Team DB posts.

This PowerPoint presentation, with annotated notes, should be posted in the Final Team Project discussion area by Sunday evening.

For this assignment, use the following format to help organize your presentation:

Final Group Project Format

The key is to provide the future direction for your business based on the outcome of the Marketplace Simulation results from Quarter 4 and connect your strategy with the course concepts learned in GB500. As a group, lay the foundation in the beginning so your classmates understand your strategy for the simulation and then discuss where you believe your company should go from here. Within the slides, incorporate discussion in the Notes section that includes American Psychological Association citations and connections to specific course materials.

To organize the PowerPoint presentation, use the format below:

1. Title Slide—include the name of your business and each group members' names (1 slide);
2. Introduction slide—discuss the company you developed and the strategy that you decided upon in the first quarter (1 slide);
3. Current situation—discuss the state of your business after the fourth quarter decisions were made. What was the position of your company in relation to each of the business functions decided each week? (1–2 slides);
4. Analysis of What Doesn't Work—explain what your team learned from the simulation related to the decisions that were made and what you would change if you could do it again (1–2 slides);
5. Direction to take—based on your strategy and current situation after quarter four decisions, discuss what direction you believe your company should take in the future and why. Be sure to include all of the business functions decided each week in the simulation (6–10 slides);
   - Include details about what you will do with sales, marketing (price, promotion, distribution, product), expansion/growth, R&D, human resources (sales force, compensation, etc.), production, et cetera and how your suggestions will affect your bottom line.
   - Support your strategy with numbers when possible.
   - Further explain your bullet points in the notes section below the slide using APA citations to course materials.
6. Conclusion—wrap up your presentation with how you believe these changes and/or strategy will help make your business as successful as it can be (1 slide);
7. References—Include the full references cited within the presentation (1 slide).

Your PowerPoint presentation will likely be between 12–15 slides, give or take a few. Do not write in paragraph form on the slides. Remember that PPT presentations are bullet points, so be clear and concise as others do not get the benefit of your additional comments. In the Notes Section of the slides, be sure to expand your thoughts using American Psychological Association citations to reference the course materials. This is the area to explain further the bullet points.

EXAMINING THE RELATIONSHIP BETWEEN VIRTUAL SCHOOL SIZE AND STUDENT ACHIEVEMENT

Sherrill Waddell

Virtual schools are a growing field in education. The growth reflects the spreading understanding that online courses and programs can serve a wide variety of students and needs (Watson & Gemin, 2009). The demand is continuing for expansion of online programs (Manzo, 2009). This past decade has seen a steady increase in the number of students selecting this form of instruction. With this growth comes the burden of establishing adequate school sizes in an effort to help students perform well both in their classes and on state testing. According to the Projections of Education Statistics to 2021 (Hussar & Bailey, 2013), total public and private elementary and secondary school enrollment was 55 million in fall 2010, representing a 6% increase since fall 1996. The International Association for K–12 Online Learning states that online learning in K–12 schools is growing explosively (iNACOL, 2009). The major appeal for many students in choosing this type of education is the flexibility that is offered from the comfort and safety of their home. Included are benefits of fewer distractions that interrupt instructional time, working at the student's own pace, and being able to travel without negative consequences in school. Online education has the potential to bring quality education to those students who may not be able to find it in a traditional classroom (Mills, 2011).

Enrollment in K–12 online learning is growing at an exponential rate throughout the United States. Currently, all 50 states offer K–12 online learning (Kennedy & Archambault, 2012). Educational institutions need to understand how to best support their students throughout their educational careers and provide the best training to prepare a 21st century workforce (Hanasky, 2010). Virtual schools are not the answer for improving schools, but they are an important addition that augments the available resources for schools. Virtual schooling is more of a hybrid of public, charter, and home schooling, with ample dashes of tutoring and independent study thrown in, all turbocharged by Internet technology (Greenway & Vanourek, 2006).

• **Sherrill Waddell**, Plantation, FL. E-mail: sherrill.waddell@gmail.com

The Quarterly Review of Distance Education, Volume 18(4), 2017, pp. 23–35   ISSN 1528-3518

RESEARCH PROBLEM

The trend and demand for virtual education has grown nationwide (McNally, 2012). With an increase in students choosing this type of education, inevitably the demand for schools of this type of educational instruction has increased in number. The purpose of this study was to determine the extent of the relationship between virtual school size and student achievement in virtual schools in a southwestern state. For the purpose of this study, achievement was measured by student performance on state testing scores. The study used descriptive and inferential statistics to analyze enrollment size and State of Texas Assessments of Academic Readiness (STAAR) English Language Arts/Reading in Grades 5 and 8, Math in Grades 5 and 8, English I, English II, and Algebra I testing scores in regard to race and gender.

THEORETICAL FRAMEWORK

The theoretical framework used for this study is the economies of scale. Marshall (1961) referred to the advantages of production on a large scale as economies of skill, economies of machinery, and economies of supplies. This basic description includes three concepts that reduce the average cost per unit through an increase in overall production efficiency. Economies of scale are often cited in education literature as being one of the drivers for the deployment of e-learning. They are used to support the notions that policy toward e-learning should promote scale efficiencies, that larger institutions will be better able to compete in the future, and that there should be substantial investment in the development of e-learning materials and online courses (Morris, 2008).

All virtual schools used in this study were managed by private companies that operate for a profit but are categorized as public schools through charter school agreements. In this study, the economies of scale theory was used

to determine the extent of the relationship between virtual school size and student achievement in virtual schools in a southwestern state.

DEFICIENCIES IN THE EVIDENCE

For the purpose of this study, student achievement was determined by a student's ability to obtain a minimum passing score on statewide testing of general standards. Student preference in choosing which virtual school to attend can be based on several characteristics of the school, including school size. Few studies have been conducted to determine the overall effectiveness and impact on student achievement that occurs as a result of students in Grades 6 to 12 taking courses through an online platform (McNally, 2012). Though numerous studies have been performed on school size in this southwestern state, this researcher was not able to find any virtual school size studies for this state. Moreover, the research on virtual school size in general is limited.

There is controversy over whether small, medium, or large schools are the most effective. Although a plethora of reforms has been suggested to improve U.S. high schools, in urban districts, the small school reform model is particularly popular (Iatarola, Schwartz, Stiefel, & Chellman, 2008). Furthermore, technology has opened up new pathways for small schools to provide rigorous curriculum through online instruction (Wu, Hsu, & Hwang, 2008).

Conversely, large school benefits include being able to hire well qualified teachers, more access to technology, and facilities that may impact student achievement (Zoda, Slate, & Combs, 2011). These researchers examined Texas elementary brick-and-mortar school size and its effect on student performance in reading, writing, and math. They reported students enrolled in large schools demonstrated higher student achievement on the Texas Assessment of Knowledge and Skills Reading,

Math, and Writing examinations compared to students enrolled in small or very small elementary schools.

It could be debated whether or not size in a virtual school has an impact on student achievement or even whether it matters, since students do not attend an actual building. Simonson (2004) states that a group made up mostly of administrators believes distance education courses do not require a classroom, and one course can have dozens, even hundreds, of students enrolled. While an abundance of research is available discussing relationships of brick-and-mortar school size and its effect on student achievement, there is a limited quantity of academic discussion and information available in regard to the virtual setting. This study of school size and its effect on student achievement in virtual schools was an attempt to add to the literature and bridge the chasm between the virtual and brick-and-mortar learning environments.

PURPOSE OF THE STUDY

The purpose of this study was to determine the extent of the relationship between virtual school size and student achievement in virtual schools in a southwestern state. For the purpose of this study, achievement was measured by student performance on state testing scores. The study used descriptive and inferential statistics to analyze enrollment size and STAAR English Language Arts/Reading in Grades 5 and 8, Math in Grades 5 and 8, English I, English II, and Algebra I testing scores in regard to race and gender.

PARTICIPANTS

The data for this research project were collected from the state education website. The target population was students who attended virtual schools in a southwestern state in the 2013–2016 school years. Students testing in Grades 5 and 8 for math and reading and students testing in Grades 9 to 12 for English I,

English II, and Algebra I comprised the target population. Four public virtual schools ranging in enrollment from 108 to 6,477 students in a southwestern state housed the target population (Texas Educational Agency [TEA], 2017a).

According to the state's Texas Academic Performance Reports (TAPR), the racial breakdown of students was categorized as African American, Hispanic, White, American Indian, Asian, Pacific Islander, and two or more races. For the purposes of this research study, the following racial categories were used: Black, Caucasian, Hispanic, American Indian, Asian, Pacific Islander, and two or more races. The data for each school were obtained by retrieving the school's TAPR for the 2013–16 school years from the state education website.

For the 2015–16 school year, all virtual schools reported students enrolled. Table 1 reveals the total number of enrolled students in the four virtual schools that were researched in this study. Schools 5 and 6 were omitted from the study because they were evaluated using an alternative accountability rating. School 4 enrollment numbers were tabulated by combining elementary, middle, and high school data from the TAPR report for the year.

Table 2 reveals the number of students enrolled in School 1 for the 2013–16 school years. As indicated above, School 1 was established in the 2013–14 school year. This school has the second fewest number of students enrolled for every year that was evaluated.

Table 3 reveals the number of students enrolled in School 2 for the 2013–16 school years. School 2 was established in the 2008–2009 school year. This school has the highest number of students enrolled for the 2013–14 and 2014–2015 school years.

Table 4 reveals the number of students enrolled in School 3 for the 2013–16 school years. School 3 was established in the 2008–2009 school year. This school has the highest number of students enrolled for the 2015–2016

TABLE 1
2013–16 Total Number of Students Enrolled in Virtual Schools in a Southwestern State

Virtual School	2013–2014	2014–2015	2015–2016
School 1	108	246	379
School 2	5,999	6,477	3,324
School 3	3,887	4,443	5,106
School 4	125	185	658

Note: The above data were retrieved from TEA (2017a), TAPR for the individual schools for 2013–2016.

TABLE 2
School 1 Number of Enrolled Students and Percentage by Grade Level and Year

School Year and Grade Level	2013–2014		2014–2015		2015–2016	
	Number	Percentage	Number	Percentage	Number	Percentage
Grade 4	0	0.0	0	0	10	2.6
Grade 5	0	0.0	11	4.5	14	3.7
Grade 6	14	13.0	19	7.7	24	6.3
Grade 7	18	16.7	33	13.4	50	13.2
Grade 8	24	22.2	44	17.9	52	13.7
Grade 9	21	19.4	41	16.7	61	16.1
Grade 10	17	15.7	44	17.9	60	15.8
Grade 11	14	13.0	32	13.0	62	16.4
Grade 12	0	0.0	22	8.9	46	12.1

Note: The above data were retrieved from TEA (2017a), TAPR for School 1.

TABLE 3
School 2 Number of Enrolled Students and Percentage by Grade Level and Year

School Year and Grade Level	2013–2014		2014–2015		2015–2016	
	Number	Percentage	Number	Percentage	Number	Percentage
Grade 2	0	0.0	1	0.0	0	0.0
Grade 3	235	3.9	228	3.5	213	6.4
Grade 4	301	5.0	381	5.9	358	10.8
Grade 5	516	8.6	499	7.7	395	11.9
Grade 6	573	9.6	612	9.4	603	18.1
Grade 7	873	14.6	769	11.9	811	24.4
Grade 8	982	16.4	1,068	16.5	944	28.4
Grade 9	1,070	17.8	1,072	16.6	0	0.0
Grade 10	669	11.2	832	12.8	0	0.0
Grade 11	524	8.7	671	10.4	0	0.0
Grade 12	256	4.3	344	5.3	0	0.0

Note: The above data were retrieved from TEA (2017a), TAPR for School 2.

TABLE 4
School 3 Number of Enrolled Students and Percentage by Grade Level and Year

School Year and Grade Level	2013–2014		2014–2015		2015–2016	
	Number	Percentage	Number	Percentage	Number	Percentage
Grade 3	136	3.5	149	3.4	153	3.0
Grade 4	212	5.5	204	4.6	203	4.0
Grade 5	282	7.3	249	5.6	269	5.3
Grade 6	337	8.7	345	7.8	351	6.9
Grade 7	487	12.5	393	8.8	456	8.9
Grade 8	645	16.6	577	13.0	586	11.5
Grade 9	572	14.7	723	16.3	966	18.9
Grade 10	746	19.2	797	17.9	841	16.5
Grade 11	299	7.7	674	15.2	794	15.6
Grade 12	171	4.4	332	7.5	487	9.5

Note: The above data were retrieved from TEA (2017a), TAPR for School 3.

TABLE 5
School 4 Number of Enrolled Students and Percentage by Grade Level and Year

School Year and Grade Level	2013–2014		2014–2015		2015–2016	
	Number	Percentage	Number	Percentage	Number	Percentage
Grade 3	5	3.96	1	.54	23	3.50
Grade 4	4	3.17	13	7.03	43	6.53
Grade 5	5	3.96	3	1.62	52	7.90
Grade 6	6	4.76	7	3.78	61	9.27
Grade 7	17	13.29	20	10.81	82	12.46
Grade 8	13	11.11	20	10.81	96	14.59
Grade 9	27	21.43	41	22.16	80	12.16
Grade 10	19	15.08	38	20.54	93	14.13
Grade 11	13	10.32	27	14.59	83	12.61
Grade 12	16	12.70	15	8.11	45	6.84

Note: The above data were retrieved from TEA (2017a), TAPR for School 4.

school year. This school has the second highest number of students enrolled for the three school years that were studied.

Table 5 reveals the number of students enrolled in School 4 for the 2013–16 school years. School 4 was established in the 2013–14 school year. This school has the third fewest students enrolled. Data for this virtual school were reported separately by school level into the TAPR system. For the purpose of this study, the information was compiled into one school.

INSTRUMENTS

The state assessments continue to be based on the TEKS, the standards designed to prepare students to succeed in college and careers and to compete globally (TEA, 2017d). However, consistent with a growing national consensus regarding the need to provide a more clearly articulated K–16 education program that focuses on fewer skills and addresses those skills in a deeper manner, the TEA is implementing a new assessment model for the

STAAR tests for elementary, middle, and high school (TEA, 2017c). The source of data for this study is results from the STAAR.

According to the education agency for this state (TEA, 2017b), Texas provides annual academic accountability ratings to its public school districts, charters, and schools. The ratings are based largely on performance on state standardized tests and graduation rates. The ratings examine student achievement, student progress, efforts to close the achievement gap, and postsecondary readiness. The state accountability system assigns one of three academic ratings to each district and campus: Met Standard, Met Alternative Standard, or Improvement Required. Below is a description of individual tests for the STAAR testing program that were used in this study according to TEA (2017b).

DEMOGRAPHIC CHARACTERISTICS

The racial breakdown of students is categorized as Black, Hispanic, White, American Indian, Asian, Pacific Islander, and Two or more races. For the purposes of this research study, the following racial categories were used: Black, Hispanic, Caucasian, Asian, and Two or more races. The categories of American Indian and Pacific Islander were not used because there was not enough representation amongst the schools for these groups. Gender is categorized by male and female. No other demographic information was included in this study.

Table 6 shows the total racial distribution of students enrolled in Southwestern state virtual schools in 2013–14. Table 7 shows the total gender distribution of students enrolled in Southwestern state virtual schools in 2013–16.

DATA ANALYSIS

In order to test the research questions, the achievement percentages and the student sample sizes were averaged across the 3 school years studied within each ethnic group. Data on achievement within the two smaller schools was limited, so, to increase the power of the

TABLE 6

2013–2016 Total Racial Distribution of Students Enrolled in Virtual Schools in a Southwestern State

Virtual School	Black	Caucasian	Hispanic	American Indian	Asian	Pacific Islander	Two or More Races
School 1	41	529	87	1	27	2	46
School 2	1,863	8,252	4,514	85	438	28	620
School 3	1,495	7,280	3,590	131	412	63	475
School 4	98	508	272	5	43	3	39

Note: The above data were retrieved from TEA (2017a), TAPR for the individual schools for 2013–2014.

TABLE 7

2013–2016 Total Gender Distribution of Students in Virtual Schools in a Southwestern State

Virtual School	Male	Female
School 1	278	455
School 2	7,045	8,755
School 3	5,427	8,016
School 4	443	746

Note: The above data were retrieved from TEA (2017a) website for the individual schools for 2014–2015.

comparisons, virtual school size was operationalized by grouping together the two schools with more than 3,000 students enrolled, and by grouping together the two schools with under 1,000 students enrolled. The average achievement percentages representing all 3 years were again averaged across the two smaller schools and across the two larger schools within each racial group. The average number of students representing all 3 years were summed across the two smaller schools and across the two larger schools within each racial group. Finally, the achievement percentages were averaged across all racial groups, and the numbers of students represented were summed across all racial groups to create overall achievement data representing all racial groups and all school years.

Achievement percentages were not available for all years within each racial group, so only the average number of students represented by the existing percentages was used in the calculations. For example, achievement percentages were only available for Black students in School 4 during the 2015–2016 school year, and no data were available on Black students in School 1 during any of the 3 years. Therefore, the small school achievement percentages for Black students across all years were represented by School 4 achievement percentages for Black students in the 2015–2016 school year, and the associated sample size was represented by the 68 Black students attending School 4 during the 2015–2016 school year.

Once achievement data had been compiled according to the protocols detailed above, z tests were computed to compare the achievement percentages between the smaller versus the larger schools within each racial group and across all racial groups combined. The overall results to address the main components of the research questions are presented in Table 8.

Parallel analyses were computed within each racial group, and are presented in Tables 9 through 13.

FINDINGS

In general, the students in the smaller schools performed significantly better across the 3 school years ($p < .001$). There were a few exceptions. Tables 9, 12, and 13 reflect the fact that even after combining the two smaller schools, sufficient data were sometimes not available for comparisons between the larger and smaller schools. In addition, it is possible that the nonsignificant results shown in Tables 11, 12, and 13 are due to the small number of students representing the smaller virtual schools.

Research Question

What is the relationship between virtual school size and students' academic achievement in STAAR English Language Arts/ Reading in Grades 5 and 8, Math in Grades 5 and 8, English I, English II, and Algebra I testing scores relating to race? In all testing categories, students performed better in small virtual schools compared to large virtual schools.

RQ1a. What is the relationship between virtual school size and students' academic success in STAAR English Language Arts/ Reading in Grades 5 and 8, Math in Grades 5 and 8, English I, English II, and Algebra I when race is concerned? In all testing categories, students performed better in small virtual schools compared to large virtual schools in all racial categories.

RQ1b. What is the relationship between virtual school size and students' academic success in STAAR English Language Arts/ Reading in Grades 5 and 8, Math in Grades 5 and 8, English I, English II, and Algebra I when gender is concerned? Conducting a statistical analysis concerning student achievement and gender was not possible, as the student achievement data were only aggregated by racial categories. It was determined that there are more females than males in all schools represented.

TABLE 8

Comparison of Large Versus Small School STAAR Percentage
at Phase-In Satisfactory Standard or Above All Grades for 2013–2016

Test	Large Schools		Small Schools		z	p <
	%	N	%	N		
Read 5	82.3	9,646	100.0	628	−11.5	0.001
Math 5	66.7	9,075	92.3	849	−15.4	0.001
Read 8	91.1	9,646	98.9	369	−5.3	0.001
Math 8	74.6	9,062	84.2	327	−3.9	0.001
English I	77.7	9,712	96.1	643	−11.1	0.001
English II	78.7	9,799	96.3	661	−10.9	0.001
Algebra I	72.5	9,712	91.3	560	−9.8	0.001

TABLE 9

Comparison of Large Versus Small School STAAR Percentage
at Phase-In Satisfactory Standard or Above All Grades for 2013–2016 for Black Students

Test	Large Schools		Small Schools		z	p <
	%	N	%	N		
Read 5	71.3	1,119	100.0	68	−5.2	0.001
Math 5	43.8	1,060	100.0	68	−9.0	0.001
Read 8	88.0	1,119				
Math 8	56.8	1,060				
English I	68.3	1,119	100.0	68	−5.5	0.001
English II	65.2	1,206	100.0	68	−5.9	0.001
Algebra I	59.3	1,119	100.0	68	−6.7	0.001

TABLE 10

Comparison of Large Versus Small School STAAR Percentage
at Phase-In Satisfactory Standard or Above All Grades for 2013–2016 for Caucasian Students

Test	Large Schools		Small Schools		z	p <
	%	N	%	N		
Read 5	84.0	5,177	100.0	442	−9.1	0.001
Math 5	71.8	4,851	97.0	599	−13.4	0.001
Read 8	90.8	5,177	97.8	264	−3.9	0.001
Math 8	72.3	4,851	86.7	246	−5.0	0.001
English I	73.7	5,177	89.0	395	−6.8	0.001
English II	79.0	5,177	92.6	395	−6.5	0.001
Algebra I	72.2	5,177	91.0	322	−7.4	0.001

Interpretation of Findings

It was unanticipated to find the results unilaterally revealing small virtual schools outperforming their counterpart of larger virtual schools in all categories. Notable trends were revealed in this study. First, small virtual schools outperform large virtual schools in academic achievement. Second, female students outnumber male students. Third, virtual

TABLE 11

Comparison of Large Versus Small School STAAR Percentage
at Phase-In Satisfactory Standard or Above All Grades for 2013–2016 for Caucasian Students

| Test | Large Schools | | Small Schools | | | |
	%	N	%	N	z	p <
Read 5	83.5	2,701	100.0	118	−4.8	0.001
Math 5	59.5	2,530	80.0	182	−5.5	0.001
Read 8	89.8	2,701	100.0	105	−3.4	0.001
Math 8	71.0	2,530	80.0	52	−1.4	NS
English I	72.5	2,701	91.5	118	−4.6	0.001
English II	77.3	2,701	92.7	170	−4.7	0.001
Algebra I	66.2	2,701	83.0	170	−4.5	0.001

TABLE 12

Comparison of Large Versus Small School STAAR Percentage
at Phase-in Satisfactory Standard or Above All Grades for 2013–2016 for Asian Students

| Test | Large Schools | | Small Schools | | | |
	%	N	%	N	z	p <
Read 5	91.2	283				
Math 5	97.0	269				
Read 8	98.0	283				
Math 8	94.5	269				
English I	96.0	294	100.0	34	−1.2	NS
English II	94.8	294				
Algebra I	92.6	294				

TABLE 13

Comparison of Large Versus Small School STAAR Percentage
at Phase-in Satisfactory Standard or Above All Grades for 2013–2016 Multiracial Students

| Test | Large Schools | | Small Schools | | | |
	%	N	%	N	z	p <
Read 5	81.4	365				
Math 5	61.7	366				
Read 8	88.7	365				
Math 8	78.5	353	86.0	29	−1.0	NS
English I	78.0	420	100.0	29	−2.8	0.01
English II	77.4	420	100.0	29	−2.9	0.01
Algebra I	72.4	420				

schools are growing in demand. There was an increase in student population for all three school years and for all four virtual schools in this study.

Context of Findings

The results of this study align with prior studies that indicate small schools surpass large schools. Carbaugh (2017) states small school benefits consist of ease in developing student to student relationships, staff familiarity with each other and the students, teachers accepting more responsibility for student learning, a stronger sense of community, and encouragement of better teaching, all of which indirectly impact student achievement and affect (Leithwood & Jantzi, 2009). As mentioned in the literature review, the Matthew Project (Friedkin, & Necochea, 1988) found that school performance benefited from smaller school size in impoverished California communities. This study did not take into consideration poverty or economically disadvantaged categories.

Implications of Findings

The intent of this study was to examine the relationship between virtual school size and student achievement. Despite the limited sample size of four virtual schools, it is evident from the results that small virtual schools are outperforming large virtual schools. As noted above, virtual schools are growing in the number of students enrolled each year. Virtual education has the potential not only to help solve many of the most pressing issues in K–12 education, but to do so in a cost-effective manner (Dillon & Tucker, 2011). More than 1 million public-education students now take online courses, and as more districts and states initiate and expand online offerings, the numbers continue to grow (Dillon & Tucker, 2011). Further research and practice could verify whether or not the trends found in this study are isolated to this specific state or if they are regional or nationwide.

The strongest argument for large schools is funding; it helps districts maintain costs while educating a large number of students. Classroom quality and school characteristics predicted youth functioning regardless of school type, reshaping the research and policy debate with renewed focus on classroom quality and school size instead of grade organization (Holas & Huston, 2012). This study helps to support the notion that small schools are better

than large schools. Even though districts could save money by investing in large schools, small schools could benefit concerning student achievement outcomes.

Limitations of the Study

This study was limited to virtual schools in a single southwestern state. At present, there are only six public virtual schools in the state, and only four were used to ensure the integrity of the study. Schools 5 and 6 were omitted from the study because they were evaluated using an alternative accountability rating. The data collected were specific to the state and may not be representative of other states. Other mitigating factors of socioeconomic status, English language learners status, special education rate, mobility rate, dropout rate, class size, instructional expenditure per pupil, or attendance rate exhibiting interaction effects can be used to predict student achievement (Riggen, 2013). They were not evaluated in this study. Assessment results can be most helpful if considered as one component of an evaluation system (TEA, 2017e). Data collected for this study were retrieved solely from the state education website using assessment results and other reporting criteria from archival data for the 2013–2016 school years. According to TEA (2017b), standardized assessments are a valuable tool for evaluating programs. However, any assessment can furnish only one part of the picture (TEA, 2017b). The STAAR end-of-course assessments are not able to identify, let alone measure, every factor that contributes to the success or failure of a program (TEA, 2017b).

Furthermore, all data collected were retrieved from the state's education website. In large-scale assessments, such as statewide testing programs, there are many steps involved in the measurement and reporting of student achievement (Wu, 2010). There may be sources of inaccuracies in each of the steps (Wu, 2010). The accuracy of reporting is dependent on individual virtual schools.

FUTURE RESEARCH DIRECTIONS

The debate regarding school size will continue in the years to come, especially as virtual schools grow. There is little research or publicly available data on the outcomes from K–12 online learning (Dillon & Tucker, 2011). This researcher was unable to obtain any relevant literature based on virtual school size and its relationship to student achievement for public virtual schools in the K–12 sector. Further research regarding virtual school size and academic achievement could include not only a single state, but include regions or an in-depth study of the entire country. Also, this study only analyzed data according to student achievement results and race. Gender data were observed based on the number of each category. Additionally, studies could explore other important factors such as graduation rates, economically disadvantaged students, and student-to-teacher ratios. Future research could explore other types of research, including a comparison study reviewing the academic achievements in virtual schools to brick-and-mortar schools that could assist lawmakers and legislatures in decisions regarding funding.

SUMMARY

The results revealed in this study indicate students in the smaller schools performed significantly better across the three school years. The study analyzed enrollment size and STAAR English Language Arts/Reading in Grades 5 and 8, Math in Grades 5 and 8, English I,

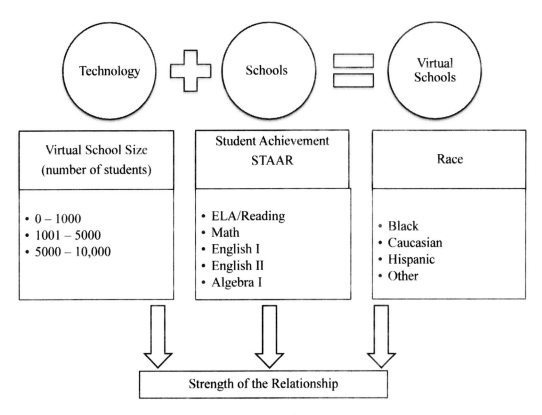

FIGURE 1

Conceptual Framework: Examining the Relationship Between Virtual School Size and Student Achievement

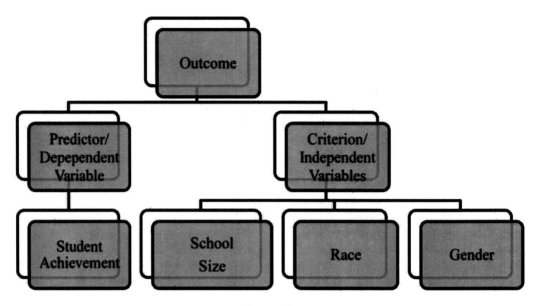

FIGURE 2
Predictor Variables and Criterion Variables Revealing Outcome

English II, and Algebra I testing scores relating to race. In all categories of both test category and race, students in smaller schools performed better than students in larger virtual schools. Notable trends were revealed in this study. First, small virtual schools outperform large virtual schools in academic achievement. Second, female students outnumber male students. Third, virtual schools are growing in demand. There was an increase in student population for all three school years and for all four virtual schools in this study.

REFERENCES

Carbaugh, E. (2017). Albamarle County Schools. *Effects of school size on student outcomes: A brief overview of research*. Retrieved from http://esblogin.k12albemarle.org/attachments/4e78e3a8-d449-42a0-a1aa-e48869e4d1de.pdf

Dillon, E., & Tucker, B. (2011). Lessons for online learning: Charter schools' successes and mistakes have a lot to teach virtual educators. *Education Next, 11*(2), 50–57.

Friedkin, N. E., & Necochea, J. (1988). School system size and performance: A contingency perspective. *Educational Evaluation and Policy Analysis, 10*(3), 237–249.

Greenway, R., & Vanourek, G. (2006). The virtual revolution: Understanding online schools. *Education Next, 6*(2), 34–41.

Hanasky, W. (2010). *Virtual programs and their impact on Appalachian Ohio high schools* (Doctoral dissertation) (Order No. 3420369). Available from ProQuest Central: ProQuest Dissertations & Theses Global. (749230473)

Holas, I., & Huston, A. C. (2012). Are middle schools harmful? The role of transition timing, classroom quality and school characteristics. *Journal of Youth and Adolescence, 41*(3), 333–345.

Hussar, W. J., & Bailey, T. M. (2013). Projection of education statistics to 2021. Retrieved from http://nces.ed.gov/pubs2013/2013008.pdf

Iatarola, P., Schwartz, A. E., Stiefel, L., & Chellman, C. C. (2008). Small schools, large districts: Small-school reform and New York City's students. *Teachers College Record, 110*(9), 1837–1878.

iNACOL (2009). Fast facts about online learning. Retrieved from http://www.inacol.org/resource/fast-facts-about-online-learning/

Kennedy, K., & Archambault, L. (2012). Offering preservice teachers field experiences in K–12 online learning: A national survey of teacher education programs. *Journal of Teacher Education 63*(3), 185–200. Retrieved from http://journals.sagepub.com/doi/abs/10.1177/0022487111433651

Leithwood, K., & Jantzi, D. (2009). A review of empirical evidence about school size effects: A policy perspective. *Review of Educational Research, 79*(1), 464–490.

Manzo, K. K. (2009). Fla. budget threatens online ed. mandate. *Education Week, 28*(30), 1, 12–13.

Marshall, A. (1961). *Principles of economics*. New York, NY: Macmillan for the Royal Economic Society.

McNally, S. R. (2012). *The effectiveness of Florida virtual school in terms of cost and student achievement in a selected Florida school district* (Doctoral dissertation). Available from ProQuest Dissertations & Theses Global: Social Sciences. (Order No. 3569631)

Mills, C. R., (2011). *Online & virtual education [electronic resource]: Its effectiveness impact on high school mathematics and science students* (Doctoral dissertation). Retrieved from http://scholarworks.montana.edu/xmlui/handle/1/1880

Morris, D. (2008). Economies of scale and scope in E-learning. *Studies in Higher Education, 33*(3), 331–343.

Riggen, V. (2013). *School size and student achievement* (Doctoral dissertation). Available from ProQuest Dissertations & Theses Global: Social Sciences. (Order No. 3589555)

Simonson, M. (2004). Class size: Where is the research? *Distance Learning, 1*(4), 56.

Sorting through online learning options: A guide for parents. (2009). Vienna, VA: International Association for K–12 Online Learning. Retrieved from https://www.inacol.org/resource/sorting-through-online-learning-options-a-guide-for-parents/

Texas Educational Agency. (2017a). School report cards. Retrieved from http://tea.texas.gov/perfreport/src/index.html

Texas Educational Agency. (2017b). Student testing and accountability. Retrieved from http://tea.texas.gov/Student_Testing_and_Accountability/Testing/

Texas Educational Agency. (2017c). State of Texas assessments of academic readiness. Retrieved from http://tea.texas.gov/student.assessment/staar/

Texas Educational Agency. (2017d). Texas essential knowledge and skills. Retrieved from http://tea.texas.gov/curriculum/teks/

Texas Educational Agency. (2017e). Student testing and accountability. Retrieved from http://tea.texas.gov/Student_Testing_and_Accountability/Testing/

Watson, J., & Gemin, B. (2009). *Management and operations of online programs: Ensuring quality and accountability. Promising practices in online learning.* Vienna, VA: International Association for K–12 Online Learning.

Wu, M. (2010). Measurement, sampling, and equating errors in large-scale assessments. *Educational Measurement, Issues and Practice, 29*(4), 15.

Wu, H., Hsu, Y., & Hwang, F. (2008). Factors affecting teachers' adoption of technology in classrooms: Does school size matter? *International Journal of Science and Mathematics Education, 6*(1), 63–85.

Zoda, P., Slate, J. R., & Combs, J. P. (2011). Public school size and Hispanic student achievement in Texas: A 5-year analysis. *Educational Research for Policy and Practice, 10*(3), 171–188.

THE USE OF E-LEARNING IN HIGHLY DOMAIN-SPECIFIC SETTINGS:
Perceptions of Female Students and Faculty in Saudi Arabia

Ayshah Alahmari
Illinois State University

Ray J. Amirault
Illinois State University

This study examines the general perceptions of Saudi Arabian faculty members and Saudi female students toward e-learning, as well as their perceptions toward potentially replacing the current closed-circuit distance technology in use for female students studying at Princess Nourah Bint Abdulrahman University (PNU) in Riyadh, Saudi Arabia, with an online, learning management system-based technology. Data were collected during spring 2016 using an online survey at PNU in Saudi Arabia (*n* = 204 female students and *n* =102 faculty members). An analysis of the data revealed that the majority of participants held positive perceptions toward the use of e-learning were it to be implemented at PNU. The study also revealed high levels of support within these groups for the implementation of e-learning-based course delivery in the case when male instructors teach and interact with female students, a common practice in Saudi Arabian higher education. After presenting the study's findings, several proposed recommendations are developed and presented for use by both decision-makers at Princess Nourah Bint Abdulrahman University and at other universities in Saudi Arabia operating under similar cultural and organizational circumstances.

INTRODUCTION

Saudi Arabia is a monarchy in the Middle East, with a population of more than 30 million. As one of the world's largest oil producers, petroleum products accounted for 85% of the country's total export revenues in 2015 (OPEC 2016). A large portion of these oil revenues has traditionally been spent on infrastructure, which includes improved educational facilities (Algarni & Male, 2014; Al-Seghayer, 2011). According to Human Development Reports (2013), 5.6% of Saudi Arabia's gross domestic product were apportioned to education expen-

• **Ayshah Alahmari**, Illinois State University. E-mail: aalahma@ilstu.edu

The Quarterly Review of Distance Education, Volume 18(4), 2017, pp. 37–56
Copyright © 2017 Information Age Publishing, Inc.

ISSN 1528-3518

ditures in 2012. Recently, Saudi Arabia dedicated $57.9 billion to education from its 2015 allocation (U.S.-Saudi Arabian Business Council, 2015). Through this income, Saudi Arabia has long been able to provide free education to its citizens from primary school through higher education (Aljabre, 2012).

Mirroring the technology revolution of the late 20th century, however, Saudi Arabian higher education has undergone significant pressures to change and adopt modern, technology-based educational delivery. The emergence of advanced, computer and Internet-based instructional technology has influenced teaching and learning within Saudi Arabia, and the Saudi government now makes it compulsory for educational institutions to be fully prepared to address these new learning trends supported by technology (Al-Asmari & Khan, 2014). A significant increase in the budget of the Ministry of Higher Education in the mid-2010s, when the price of the oil dramatically increased (Alamri, 2011; Aljabre, 2012), was designed to support such goals.

In Saudi Arabia, there are only some 25 public universities, and the estimated number of students attempting to matriculate is some 450,000 (Almutairy, Davies, & Dimitriadi, 2015). Saudi universities are therefore facing significant overcrowding (Alebaikan & Troudi, 2010; Asiri, bt Mahmud, Bakar, & bin Mohd Ayub, 2012). To put it in concrete terms, the number of enrolled Saudi students in 2005 was 151,998, but swelled to a staggering 905,892 students in 2011, a 600% increase (Baqutayan, 2011).

This enormous higher education growth trend prompted the Saudi Ministry of Higher Education to take significant steps to address the problem. The government, for example, encouraged Saudi students to study abroad via means of government-funded scholarships. As an example, the King Abdullah Scholarship Program (established in 2005) is potentially the largest government scholarship program in the world, with approximately 125,000 Saudi students studying in 23 different countries (Al Mousa, 2010; Taylor & Albasri, 2014). The

Saudi Electronic University (established in 2011) similarly was implemented to ameliorate enrollment crowding by providing blended learning to students, the first of its kind in Saudi Arabia (Asiri, 2014; Pavan, 2013).

Though the Ministry of Higher Education has begun integrating web-based instruction with its traditional instructional delivery (Alahmari & Kyei-Blankson, 2016; Alebaikan & Troudi, 2010), Saudi universities are no longer able to accommodate the large and growing number of students (Alshangeeti, Alsaghier, & Nguyen, 2009), prompting a rethink of e-learning as a potential mechanism to address the issue, particularly for the new generation of students who grew up in the digital age, the so-called "digital natives" (Almutairy et al., 2015). King Abdulaziz University was the first Saudi university to offer bachelor's degrees through online learning (Alebaikan & Troudi, 2010), and other Saudi universities, such as Al-Imam Mohammad ibn Saud Islamic University, the Arab Open University, and later, the Saudi Electronic University, have subsequently adopted e-learning programs that lead to bachelor's degrees.

Despite these programs, e-learning is being adopted at a relatively slow pace (Al-Asmari & Khan 2014; Mirza & Al-Abdulkareem, 2011), with e-learning minimally included and/or supported in higher education institutions (Alamri, 2011). A significant factor affecting slowed e-learning adoption is related to gender. Unlike most Western universities, public universities in Saudi Arabia consist of two geographically separated campuses: one campus for male students, and the other for female students. This separation is due to religious and cultural norms of the society that are upheld by governmental laws and policies (Almutairy et al., 2015; van Geel, 2016). Due to the shortage in the number of available female faculty, an ongoing need for male instructors to teach within female campus exists (Mirza, 2007). However, male instructors are authorized only to teach female students indirectly using courses that are remotely delivered by means of closed-circuit television, one-way video and two-way audio, or broadcast audio. Female students view lectures in real time via a TV monitor, and use a microphone system to ask questions and give feedback (Yamin, 2015).

Such a reality would appear tailor-made for e-learning approaches. However, online courses continue to remain of minor interest in Saudi universities due to a lack of basic knowledge and the training needed to effectively implement e-learning systems (Al-Asmari & Khan, 2014). Nevertheless, it would seem that the large and growing number of Saudi students, as well as the need for male instructors teaching within female campuses, will continue to pressure the adoption of online learning more broadly across Saudi universities. Al-Asmari and Khan (2014), for example, argue that e-learning has become an urgent need in Saudi Arabian higher education. Interestingly, no research has been conducted on the effectiveness of online education as a method for helping female Saudi students overcome learning barriers and challenges when they are taught by male instructors in Saudi universities.

Given this historical and cultural background, this study was designed to examine the potential adoption of e-learning in the specific case of Princess Nourah Bint Abdulrahman University (PNU), as well as explore the perspectives of male faculty members and female students regarding the benefits of, and barriers to, adopting e-learning-based pedagogical approaches. More specifically, this study focuses on the potential perceived benefits in replacing the currently employed closed-circuit television technology with an learning management system (LMS)-based e-learning approach when male instructors teach female students.

Research Questions

The research questions of this study are:

1. What experience, if any, do Saudi faculty members and students already possess in teaching/taking e-learning courses at PNU?
2. What are the perceived benefits of e-learning courses at PNU?
3. What are the perceived benefits of replacing closed-circuit live video with fully e-learning-based courses?
4. What barriers and challenges may prevent PNU from taking advantage of e-learning approaches?
5. To what extent are Saudi faculty and students willing to accept and embrace e-learning courses?
6. What motivational factors are required in faculty and students to move toward an e-learning-based modality?
7. What are the prevailing views on the probable and/or preferable future of e-learning in Saudi Arabia?

Although this study is focused on PNU, findings may have a broader reach into the overall Saudi university context due to the cultural and structural similarities of Saudi universities, and the fact that PNU is representative of many other Saudi universities in terms of female education and the use of distance education (e-learning) for religious and culture reasons (Yamin, 2015).

Significance of the Study

The study's results can provide significant, but different, insights to four distinct groups. First, instructors who are currently employing closed-circuit television for instruction can consider the potential benefits of shifting into an e-learning-based approach. Second, Saudi officials and educators can use the study's results to help inform them in making decisions regarding the adoption of e-learning into the Saudi national context. Third, the greater Saudi higher education context can benefit from understanding the perspectives toward e-learning of faculty and students at a major university such as PNU. Fourth, and most broadly, countries with similar cultural settings can benefit from the study by gaining an understanding of how e-learning might be received in their own national contexts. All four groups can share an enhanced understanding of both the obstacles and challenges that may prevent the effective adoption of e-learning.

Theoretical/Conceptual Framework

A country's readiness for e-learning is as much an essential part of the potential success of e-learning as is e-learning's technological implementation. Measuring the level of e-learning readiness and implementation in higher education requires clear understanding of the interaction between e-learning components, including technology, users, and the existing culture of the institution undertaking an e-learning initiative (Ouma, Awuor, & Kyambo, 2013). Akaslan and Law (2010), for example, highlight the importance of investigating the extent of the existing information and communication technology infrastructure in an institution that can support e-learning implementation. Indeed, the successful implementation of e-learning depends on the level of experience and confidence of users using various information and communication technology and their attitudes toward e-learning and its potential derived benefits (Holden & Rada, 2011). According to Mosa, Naz'ri bin Mahrin, and Ibrrahim (2016), the culture of the institution is a significant component that can affect the success of e-learning implementation. The implementation of e-learning may face resistance due to a "traditional" culture that may exist within an institution, and it is therefore essential that an institution be as fully culturally prepared as possible to maximize the potential for a successful e-learning strategy.

LITERATURE REVIEW

Many universities around the world have taken advantage of the benefits that e-learning offers (Allen & Seaman, 2015). Historically, the founding of University of South Africa in 1962 and the UK Open University in 1970 marked a major development and fundamental change in e-learning and how it was practiced (Simonson, Smaldino, Albright, & Zvacek, 2014). This significant development in the delivery of distance education was accomplished by offering a mixed-media approach, where learning materials (text, audio, and visuals) were sent to students by mail and then supplemented by broadcast radio and television (Matthews, 1999). Another significant event in the history of e-learning occurred when Turkey's Higher Education Act nominated Anadolu University in 1981 as the national Turkish provider of distance education. Its mission was to educate Turks living in rural areas and others who did not have the time (or resources) to enroll in conventional schools (MacWilliams, 2000). This mission at Anadolu University is largely viewed as successful, with enrollment increasing to "500,000 distance education students, which makes it the largest university on Earth" (MacWilliams, 2000, as cited in Simonson et al., 2014, p. 14).

The Middle East has also been involved in the furthering of e-learning as an educational mechanism. The Gulf Cooperation Council for example, consisting of members Saudi Arabia, Bahrain, Qatar, Oman, United Arab Emirates, and Kuwait, are improving education and alleviating pedagogical issues that are unique to Gulf societies, including the gender segregation factor (Weber, 2009). Along these lines, the Kingdom of Saudi Arabia has established the National Plan for Information Technology with a progressive vision to develop lifelong education (Al-Asmari & Khan, 2014; Alebaikan & Troudi, 2010). The National Plan for Information Technology in 2006 contributed in promoting e-learning across Saudi Arabia by establishing a National E-learning and Distance Learning Centre to encourage and enhance e-learning and distance education in higher education, with the goal of making education available to all individuals (Alebaikan & Troudi, 2010; Jabli & Qahmash, 2013). According to Al-Fahad (2009), the infrastructure for this e-learning and distance education initiative has already been officially established and has resulted in:

1. implementing the e-learning educational portal system *"Tajseer"*—تجسير;
2. implementing the LMS in e-learning *"Jusur"*—جسور;
3. implementing the national repository for learning objects *"Taiseer"*—تيسير;
4. creating the Saudi National Center for e-learning, and distance education for university education, which harmonizes e-learning management systems with the needs of university education in the Kingdom of Saudi Arabia; and
5. launching an award for university e-learning excellence.

In spite of these developments, Saudi Arabia remains in the early phases of accepting and adapting e-learning, even if increasing numbers of individuals are currently now recognizing its potential benefits. A significant study conducted by Al-Shehri (2010) using a qualitative approach aimed at exploring views of 30 senior academicians and decision makers about the current and future developments and challenges of e-learning in Saudi Arabia revealed that most participants believed that e-learning is inevitable in Saudi universities and were optimistic about its future. Al-Shehri identified challenges and obstacles that face e-learning in Saudi Arabia, including budgetary allocations, the ability of teachers and learners to effectively use e-learning, required infrastructure, and the organizational relationships of those involved in e-learning. Al-Shehri concluded that it is essential to prepare e-learners, and to understand their characteristics, motivations, and potential before embarking on major e-learning programs.

In a descriptive study, El Zawaidy (2014) examined the perception of 360 information technology faculty members who were using the Blackboard learning management system at three public universities in Saudi Arabia (King Saud University in Riyadh, King Khaled University in Abha, and Taif University in Taif). El Zawaidy's study attempted to identify the obstacles that face faculty members while using Blackboard. The study revealed insufficient instructor training in Blackboard functionally when used as a part of blended learning system, low quality Internet connections, and a lack of interest or motivation within faculty in improving their technology skills.

In a similar study, Bousbahi and Alrazgan (2015) investigated the perceptions of information technology faculty members about of the incorporation of LMS's into their courses in King Saud University in Saudi Arabia. In this empirical study, the researchers found that Blackboard was the only LMS used in King Saud University, and was frequently used as merely as a storage device for one-way dissemination of resources and material to students, rather than a dissemination technology enabling two-way communication. The study also reported that some faculty members viewed Blackboard as a tedious, unclear, and difficult-to-use LMS. The study also revealed that factors such as motivation and organizational support impacted information technology faculty members' acceptance of the LMS as an educational tool (Bousbahi & Al Razgan, 2015). More broadly, these studies demonstrated that most faculty members working within these educational contexts were not aware of all functionalities available within Blackboard, due to a lack of training, and the time required to explore and understand such Blackboard functionalities (Bousbahi & Al Razgan, 2015).

Mobile learning (m-learning) as a specific variant of e-learning is still in its inception phase in many developing countries. Yet, some universities in Saudi Arabia have already adopted short message service in education, including King Saud University, which recently initiated a new short message service that offers the ability to send text messages directly from a personal computer to a mobile phone (Altameem, 2011). A study conducted by Al-Fahad (2009) examined the attitudes of 186 undergraduate female students toward the effectiveness of mobile learning applied in King Saud University and found that students held positive attitudes to mobile learning and supported the possibility of expanding wireless network infrastructures to increase the flexibility of access to learning resources. In this study, Al-Fahad (2009) concluded that mobile learning is an effective tool in improving communication and learning, and that short message service technology can be used effectively to support and improve student relationships. In another study, Almutairy et al. (2015) investigated the perspective of 131 Saudi students in a pilot study at United Kingdom universities about the possibility of integrating m-learning into Saudi Arabian higher education institutions. The findings of this study imply that Saudi students are ready for using m-learning as a method to achieve personal educational aims. Almutairy et al. (2015) asserted that higher education policy makers in Saudi Arabia should consider the possibility of creating m-learning environments at academic institutions.

Furthermore, the use of LMS technology is being increasingly adopted within Saudi universities (Asiri et al., 2012). According to Alebaikan and Troudi (2010), many Saudi Arabian universities and institutions have employed different LMS's, including Blackboard, WebCT, and Tadarus (an Arabic-based LMS) to facilitate teaching and learning in higher education. However, the implementation of the blended learning approach at Saudi universities has experienced many obstacles and challenges, including the acceptance of this pedagogical approach from within a traditional university culture, determination of the optimal design of blended learning, and the time requirements for faculty to learn how best to use the technology, including time required for training workshops (Alebaikan & Troudi, 2010).

The studies referenced here reveal a somewhat sparse and insufficient literature base on the experiences and perspectives of faculty members and students in relation to their acceptance and readiness for online education in Saudi Arabia. This includes documenting deficiencies surrounding feelings about the appropriateness of replacing the closed-circuit television currently used when male professors are teaching female students at Saudi universities with online courses delivered through an LMS. This study responds to this gap in the literature by investigating these questions more directly and collecting empirical data on implementing this educational modality.

METHODOLOGY

A quantitative approach was used to examine the perspectives of the faculty members and female students about e-learning at PNU in Riyadh, Saudi Arabia and the perceived effectiveness of e-learning-based course delivery and the extent of the readiness and acceptance of e-learning-based courses to replace the closed-circuit television technology currently in use when male professors are teaching female students at PNU. A pilot of the survey was conducted during the fall semester of 2015, and resulted in 447 responses. After reviewing the data gathered from the pilot study, it was determined that the instrument was effectively collecting the data necessary for a full study. The full study's quantitative data were analyzed using SPSS, and qualitative comments were translated, reviewed, and compared against the quantitative findings for additional insight on the quantitative findings.

Participants

The target population for this study was the female student body and the faculty members at PNU in Riyadh, Saudi Arabia, estimated at 46,813 female students and 2,218 faculty members (Ministry of Education, 2015). The participants of this study ($N = 306$) consisted of 204 female PNU students and 102 PNU faculty members during the spring semester of 2016. Table 1, a description of the female student participants, reveals that most the female student participants were undergraduate stu-

TABLE 1
Description of Student Participants

	Frequency	*Percent*
Age		
20 and below	40	19
21–25	124	61
26–30	22	11
31 and above	18	9
Educational Level		
Undergraduate	177	87
Graduate	26	13

TABLE 2
Description of Faculty Participants

	Frequency	*Percent*
Age		
25 and below	2	2
26–35	55	54
36–45	31	31
46 and above	13	13
Gender		
Male	21	20
Female	81	80
Educational Level		
Bachelor's degree	31	31
Master's degree	47	46
Doctoral degree	23	23
Years of Teaching Experience		
1–3 years	55	54
4–10 years	37	37
11–20 years	7	7
21–years	2	2

dents (87%), and more than half of them (61%) were between 21 to 25 years old.

Table 2, focused on faculty demographics in this study, shows that most faculty participants were female (80%); 46% of faculty members held master's degrees, 31% held bachelor's degrees, and 23% of faculty held doctoral degrees; 54% of participating faculty ranged in age from 26–35 years, 31% 36–45 years of age, 13% 46 and above, and 2% were age 25 and below. Regarding years of teaching experience, 54% of faculty members had 1–3 years of experience, 37% 4–10 years of experi-

ence, 7% 11–20 years of experience, and 2% of faculty had more than 21 years of teaching experience.

Student learning responsibility and self-discipline is reflected in Table 3. Half of female student participants reported that they are responsible for their own learning, while 48% reported that they share an equal responsibility with their instructors for learning; 44% of female students reported that they often get things done ahead of time, while 28% reported that they need reminding to complete schoolwork, and the remain-

TABLE 3
Level of Student's Learning Responsibility and Self-Discipline

	Frequency	Percent
Learning Responsibility		
I am responsible for my own learning.	102	50
The instructor and I share equal responsibility.	97	48
The instructor is most responsible for my learning.	5	2
Self-Discipline		
Often gets things done ahead of time	90	44
Needs reminding to get things done on time	56	28
Puts off things until the last moment	58	28

TABLE 4
Technology Skills and Use

	Students		Faculty	
	N	%	N	%
1. High: I am "digitally fluent" and can learn new programs quickly.	108	53	23	23
2. Moderate: I have enough skills to complete my tasks.	94	46	47	46
3. Low: I am either a novice computer user or I really don't like using a computer.	2	1	31	31

der reported that they wait until the last moment to complete schoolwork.

Technology skills are reported in Table 4. More than half of female students (53%) considered their skills to be high, and are "digitally fluent" (i.e., can learn new programs quickly); 46% considered their skills to be moderate, and possess skills sufficient to complete their learning tasks. For faculty participants, 46% rate their technology skills to be moderate, and 31% of faculty considered their skills to be low (i.e., view themselves as a novice, and do not like using computers).

Study Procedure

Two permissions were obtained prior to conducting the study. One permission was from PNU in Saudi Arabia for purposes of contacting and collecting data from faculty members and female students. The other permission was from the Institutional Review Board at Illinois State University to participate in human subject research. Both researchers

hold current Collaborative Institutional Training Initiative certifications.

After approvals from both the PNU and Institutional Review Board, the developed survey was electronically sent to the faculty members and female students by PNU. The electronic survey invitation included an online link to the survey, which contained a consent form that detailed the purpose of the study, the steps for participation, and information about the research and researchers. The confidentiality of the participants was respected during the stages of the study by not referring to the participants by name. The survey was conducted both with volunteer participation and informed consent. Participants were informed that they could withdraw from the study at any time without penalty. No participant received an incentive or compensation for the participation.

The Survey Instrument

The electronic survey was hosted on SurveyMonkey.com. The survey was directly developed from a literature review on e-learning and online course delivery. The survey was developed in English, and then translated into the Arabic language with a certified translation service. Certified translation was used to ensure that there was no difference between the English and Arabic versions of the survey and to ensure that the participants had a good understanding of the survey items. Data collected from the survey were translated from Arabic back into English for analysis and presentation. The survey instrument was constructed in eight parts:

a. demographic information for faculty and female students;
b. technology skills;
c. experience with online learning;
d. perspectives regarding the benefits of e-learning
e. challenges to e-learning;
f. readiness and acceptance of online learning;
g. motivation to move toward e-learning; and;
h. open-ended questions for faculty members and female students to share their views on the probable/preferable future of e-learning in Saudi Arabia.

A 5-point Likert-scale collected quantitative data, ranging from 1 (*strongly disagree*) to 5 (*strongly agree*), on items b through g; item a and item f collected qualitative data.

Validity and Reliability

Validity is defined by Roberts (2010, p. 151) as "the degree to which the instrument truly measures what it purports to measure," and reliability as "the degree to which the instrument consistently measures something from one time to another." Prior to conducting the full study, a pilot study was conducted, which included testing the validity and reliability of the research instrument. To establish validity, the word choice, answer choices, and construction of each item were reviewed to determine whether each item measured its intended object. To test for reliability, a Cron-

bach's alpha was computed to verify internal consistency of the survey items. Theoretically, all reliability estimates should meet the desired standard level of 0.70 or above that is suggested by Green and Salkind (2014). According to Mohsen and Reg (2011), the higher the Cronbach's alpha, the more reliable the test results. In this study, the Cronbach's alpha was found to be 0.90.

Data Analysis

The quantitative data was analyzed with SPSS. All data collected from the surveys were analyzed using descriptive statistics including weighted averages, frequency and percentage. The weighted means of Likert items were computed to determine the trends in the responses. The study was intended to produce empirical information describing the level of readiness for implementing e-learning at PNU. Descriptive statistics were used to present the results of the statistical data analysis, and summarized results were developed for each of the first six research questions. Responses to the open-ended questions were then examined to provide additional insight into the meaning of the data.

RESULTS

eLearning at PNU

The first survey question was: "What experience, if any, do Saudi faculty members and students already possess in teaching/taking e-learning courses at PNU?" Table 6 presents findings for this question.

In addition, faculty members where asked if they have participated in any conference on e-learning and online education. Table 7 presents the findings for this question.

Perceived Benefits of E-learning

The second survey question was: "What are the perceived benefits of e-learning courses at PNU?" Table 8 shows that most female stu-

TABLE 5
Cronbach's Alpha Reliability for the Survey Subscales

Item	N	Alpha
The benefits of online courses	15	0.90
The benefits of online courses for female students taught by male instructors	6	0.89
Challenges to e-learning	11	0.83
Readiness and acceptance of e-learning	7	0.88
Motivations toward e-learning	10	0.93

TABLE 6
Experience of Taking/Teaching Online Courses

	Students		Faculty	
	N	%	N	%
Yes	68	33	11	11
No	135	67	90	89

TABLE 7
Participating in Conferences
About E-learning/Online Learning

	Frequency	Percent
Yes	19	19
No	82	81

dents and faculty participants strongly agreed that online education meets the needs of students who have difficulty attending traditional classes, such as those living far away from the university. The highest item had a mean of 4.49 for female students and 4.47 for faculty members (online courses meet the needs of students who have difficulty attending traditional classes, such as those living far away from the university).

The third survey question was: "What are the perceived benefits of replacing the closed-circuit television with fully online courses?" The results of this question are depicted in Table 9. Generally, all participants agreed or strongly agreed on all 6 items, with the mean ranging between 3.66 and 4.47. The item "Allow easier contact with the male instructor for questions and explanations at any time"

had the highest mean, at 4.10 for female students, and 4.23 for faculty members.

Perceived Barriers and Challenges to E-Learning

The fourth survey question was: "What barriers and challenges may prevent PNU from taking advantage of e-learning approaches?" The results for this question, depicted in Table 10, convey findings correlated to faculty/student responses to rate to what extent they agree on the 11 challenges to e-learning. As can be seen, female students and faculty participants agreed on most of these eleven items, with a mean that ranged between 3.42 and 4.24. The greatest perceived barriers to e-learning for faculty were the limited technological infra-

TABLE 8
Perceived General Benefits of Online Courses

	Student			Faculty		
	M	SD	N	M	SD	N
Meet the needs of students who have difficulty attending traditional classes, such as those living far away from the university	4.49	.636	196	4.47	.839	94
Help address transportation issues, particularly for Saudi women	4.29	1.072	196	4.37	.961	94
Address the issue of population growth with limited space	4.07	1.060	196	4.14	1.012	94
Cost less and free space for other purposes within the university	3.79	1.130	196	4.05	1.071	94
Permit students who failed a traditional course to take the course again online	4.06	.845	196	4.02	1.067	94
Reduce scheduling conflicts for students	4.02	.963	196	4.04	1.036	94
Offer courses not otherwise available	4.07	.977	196	3.73	1.175	94
Build important relationships with individuals from other organizations	3.88	1.091	196	3.66	1.083	94
Provide experiences that are comparable in educational value to traditional face-to-face instruction	3.71	1.082	196	3.97	.885	94
Help promote a belief in the value and legitimacy of online education in Saudi Arabia	3.95	.919	196	4.15	.867	94
Support students' self-learning skills	4.24	.797	196	4.36	.670	94
Promote students' self-regulated learning behaviors	4.26	.839	196	4.04	1.036	94
Enable students to become more engaged with their instructors	3.99	.971	196	3.85	1.057	94
Enable students to become more engaged with their classmates	3.53	1.111	196	3.82	1.173	94
Benefit students by providing opportunities to listen to audio lectures and watching video recordings at a student's own pace	4.47	.719	196	4.12	.949	94

TABLE 9
Perceived Benefits of Online Courses for Female Students

	Student			Faculty		
	M	SD	N	M	SD	N
Provide an effective interaction with the instructors while protecting the religious and cultural norms of the society	3.94	.962	202	4.14	.866	97
Allow easier contact with the male instructor for questions and explanations at any time.	4.10	.823	202	4.23	.771	97
Permits more timely instructor feedback on assignments	4.08	.880	202	4.01	.963	97
Addresses the lack of female instructors teaching within all-female campuses	3.90	1.048	202	3.99	.995	97
Fulfill many important student educational and social needs	3.91	1.001	202	3.89	1.069	97
Are more comfortable for female students by offering online course discussions rather than in-person discussions	3.92	1.171	202	3.87	1.027	97

structure to support e-learning, such as high speed Internet connections and the restrictive laws or policies which might prevent universities from supporting e-learning ($M = 4.24$). For female students, the greatest perceived barrier to e-learning was the lack of cooperation between universities in terms of the exchange of e-learning experiences ($M = 4.16$). The

TABLE 10
Perceived Challenges to E-Learning

	Student			Faculty		
	M	SD	N	M	SD	N
Limited technological infrastructure to support e-learning, such as high speed Internet connections	3.72	1.106	195	4.24	.751	59
Lack of cooperation between universities in terms of the exchange of e-learning experiences	4.16	.821	195	4.19	.776	59
Lack of financial funding	4.05	.912	195	3.93	.998	59
A shortage number of instructors who accept and support e-learning	3.87	.943	195	3.85	1.142	59
A shortage of professional technicians providing technical assistance, maintenance of equipment, and troubleshooting technical malfunctions	3.80	.982	195	3.92	1.087	59
A shortage of training courses designed to support both e-learners and e-instructors	3.64	1.096	195	3.85	1.014	59
A general perception that students require more discipline to succeed in an online course than in a face-to-face course	3.53	1.198	195	3.81	1.042	59
A general perception that e-learning is a secondary educational priority	3.42	1.187	195	3.93	.828	59
A general perception concerning the quality of the online courses	3.60	1.105	195	3.85	1.031	59
Suffer from a lack of awareness of the e-culture consisting of faculty members, students, and the broader society	3.91	.957	195	3.90	.923	59
Restrictive laws or policies which might prevent universities from supporting e-learning	3.66	.935	195	4.24	.751	59

items; "a general perception that e-learning is a secondary educational priority" ($M = 3.42$) and "a general perception that students require more discipline to succeed in an online course than in a face-to-face course" ($M = 4.81$) were the lowest reported barriers.

Perceived Readiness and Acceptance of E-Learning

The fifth survey question was: "To what extent are Saudi faculty and students willing to accept and embrace e-learning courses?" The results in this section examine the components that motivate faculty/students at PNU to accept and be ready for online education. Table 11 show that most female students and faculty participants agreed on all 7 items, with a mean ranging from 3.73 to 4.14 for female students

and from 3.99 to 4.42 for faculty. The highest mean for female students ($M = 4.14$) was on the item "easily learn new technologies and use them effectively to enhance learning." The highest mean for faculty ($M = 4.21$) was on the item "can locate solutions when I have a problem with technology." An interesting finding depicted in the previous table is that the lowest means for female students ($M = 3.59$) and faculty ($M = 4.04$) were on the same item, "prefer online courses rather than the closed-circuit television"

Perceived Motivations Toward E-learning

The sixth survey question was: "What motivational factors are required in faculty and students to move toward an e-learning-based

TABLE 11
Perceived Readiness and Acceptance of E-Learning

	Student			Faculty		
	M	*SD*	*N*	*M*	*SD*	*N*
Easily learn new technologies and use them effectively to enhance learning/ teaching	4.14	.771	203	3.99	.982	85
Can locate solutions when I have a problem with technology	3.75	1.019	203	4.21	.725	85
Enjoy using my own PC/Laptop/mobile phone for learning/ teaching	4.08	.909	203	4.12	1.040	85
Am confident when using my PC/Laptop/mobile phone for learning/teaching	4.03	.930	203	4.09	.971	85
Believe online courses increase the quality of e-learning	3.73	1.181	203	4.20	.949	85
Believe online courses provide me with new methods for learning/ teaching	3.85	1.129	203	4.12	.837	85
Prefer online courses rather than the closed-circuit television	3.59	1.128	203	4.04	.892	85

TABLE 12
Perceived Motivations Toward E-learning

	Student			Faculty		
	M	*SD*	*N*	*M*	*SD*	*N*
Availability of hardware (particularly computers)	4.26	.699	191	3.92	1.046	91
High speed Internet connectivity	4.42	.803	191	4.44	.763	91
Improved online learning management systems	4.34	.699	191	4.53	.621	91
Appropriate policies favoring e-learning	4.40	.623	191	4.47	.603	91
Technical support for my computer, my network connection, and my learning management system	4.32	.807	191	4.45	.778	91
Lower Internet connectivity prices	4.45	.662	191	4.52	.705	91
Availability of reliable electricity	4.46	.671	191	4.47	.835	91
Appropriate extra resources in the Arabic language	4.32	.731	191	4.51	.808	91
Raised awareness about the value of e-learning at both governmental and personal levels across the society	4.40	.717	191	4.53	.735	91
Professional training for the technology use	4.38	.729	191	4.56	.687	91

modality?" All mean scores were higher than 3.92, indicating that most female students and faculty agreed or strongly agreed on the 10 items, with a mean ranging between 4.26 and 4.46 for female students, and from 3.92 to 4.56 for faculty (see Table 12). The highest mean result regarding motivation toward e-learning among female students was the availability of reliable electricity (*M* = 4.46), whereas the most agreed upon motivation among faculty was the professional training for the technology use (*M* = 4.56). Faculty also strongly agreed on the need to raise awareness about the value of e-learning at both governmental and personal levels across the society (*M* = 4.53), and to improve online learning management system (*M* = 4.53).

Narrative Responses

The final portion of the survey consisted of open-ended questions developed to help shed additional light on the data collected from the quantitative data collected from the previous

Likert-style questions. Faculty members and female students were asked to share their prevailing views on the probable and/or preferable future of e-learning in Saudi Arabia.

Forty-five students and 35 faculty members provided narrative commentary on this question. A review of this qualitative data revealed that most faculty and student comments were in support of e-learning. Some of the faculty favorable comments included (translated here into English from Arabic): "It is improving and will have a bright future," "It will increase the enrollment of students who live in remote areas," and "It will get a greater attention and widespread use." Students also offered positive comments such as, "E-learning offers the opportunity for anyone [who] wants to learn," and "e-learning will replace the use of the closed-circuit television by online education due to its benefits for both male instructors and female students."

In addition to their comments, some participants submitted recommendations and/or suggestions regarding e-learning in Saudi universities. Some of faculty comments included: "E-learning will require hard work and cooperation from various institutions," "It needs to increase the awareness of the importance of self-learning for students," "The preferable future of e-learning will take [a] long time because of the old administrators who are unaware of its importance," and "The preferable future of e-learning will be achieved by providing all supplies and materials needed to support this educational style." Both faculty and students shared many concerns surrounding technological infrastructure they perceived as being particularly valuable to support e-learning in Saudi universities, such as high speed Internet with reasonable price for students, technical support, professional training programs for instructors, computer laboratories, and funding. Student participants made note of the necessity of valuing the outcomes of e-learning equally with traditional learning. Some comments of note include: "It needs to be valuable and accredited equally with the traditional education in Saudi higher education

and job market," "E-learning will be advanced in Saudi Arabia when students who are graduated from distance education have opportunities to be hired as equally as those from traditional education," and "It seems that e-learning will be limited to self-learning, but at the university level, it is more likely to disappear because it is not trusted by the job market in Saudi Arabia."

DISCUSSION

The current study was designed to sample and examine the perspectives of faculty members and female students at PNU in Saudi Arabia. Questions focused on the benefits of e-learning, the challenges to e-learning in Saudi Arabia, the readiness for, and acceptance of, e-learning, and the motivation these groups hold toward LMS-based technology as a replacement for the currently used closed-circuit television technology.

Results from this study indicated that the perspectives of the faculty and female students were generally positive toward e-learning. Respondents largely agreed or strongly agreed with the 15 statements of the benefits of e-learning and other six statements surrounding the benefits of online course delivery, particularly for female students. Faculty and female students showed high awareness of the potential benefits of e-learning to enhance current teaching and learning practice.

Online Learning for Female Students

This study provides empirical evidence that most female students possess relatively high levels of self-discipline, time commitment, and basic technology skills that are necessary for e-learning. Invariably, it is required that students have a good degree of self-discipline, self-motivation, and time commitment to be successful in e-learning (cf. Lee, 2016). The study reveals that one of the greatest perceived benefits of e-learning is its ability to meet the needs of students who have difficulty attending traditional classes, such as those living far away from the university, and in assisting in transportation issues present in Saudi Arabia, particularly for Saudi women. This finding is consistent with finding of previous studies which indicated that the shift toward e-learning is expected to empower Saudi female students in overcoming social and cultural obstacles (Alahmari, 2017; Almutairy et al., 2015). The study also provided evidence of high levels of support for replacing the closed-circuit television technology currently used by PNU and most Saudi universities with LMS-based-technology when male faculty teach female students. It is also apparent from this study that female students were in favor of taking online courses as an alternative to the closed-circuit television method. This aligns with a recent study on online learning that indicates that "online courses are becoming a more widely popular and viable option for many adult learners" (Lee, 2016, p. 81).

The analysis of the computed and narrative results of the current study showed that female students view e-learning favorably and as beneficial, which agrees with the results of previous studies cited in this study carried out in variety settings (Alturise, 2013; Jabli & Qahmash, 2013). Female students in this study reported high levels of acceptance and readiness for e-learning. The study also revealed that most female students indicated they have adequate knowledge of technology, as well as high awareness of the benefits of e-learning. In sum, the results of this study found that, overall, female students at PNU are ready for e-learning and would prefer the use of e-learning-based courses, rather than closed-circuit television approaches.

Online Learning for Faculty Members

The area found to contain the widest divergence between faculty and students was in the rating of technology skills. While most female students, for example, rated their technology skills to be "high" to "moderate," most faculty members rated their technology skills to be "moderate" to "low." This would imply that faculty members may lack the technology skills needed to incorporate technology into their teaching practice (Alfahad, 2012) and the need for increased and ongoing faculty professional development to ensure the quality and success of e-learning courses.

The results of this study revealed that most faculty reacted very favorably to the online course as a replacement for closed-circuit television modality. However, it was found that faculty participants have limited experiences with e-learning, as well as limited participation in e-learning and online education conferences. This result was largely consistent with the findings of Alebaikan and Troudi (2010), where it was found that faculty and students have not had direct experience with online learning. However, it is acknowledged that instructors' technology skills, experiences with e-learning, and their attitudes toward e-learning influence their perception of the effectiveness of the modality. Considering this, faculty participants would likely benefit from participating in professional development programs to strengthen their technology skills, and could play a crucial factor in the success of e-learning in Saudi universities. Developing training opportunities for faculty was reported as the greatest motivation in moving toward effective implementation of e-learning in Saudi universities. This, too, is in line with the findings of Al-Hattami, Muammar, and Elmahdi (2013), who reported the need of providing professional development opportunities to enhance faculty members' professional abilities in using technology. The present findings also support Al-Zahrani's (2015a) study, which concluded that the training opportunities provided to faculty in terms of information and communication technologies were inadequate, reporting the need for continued training through group training, individual training, and self-training.

Challenges to E-Learning

This study also highlighted challenges that might prevent the success of e-learning-based education at PNU. The greatest reported perceived challenge was the limited technological infrastructure to support e-learning, including Internet connections, technical support, computer laboratories, digital resources, and use of appropriate LMS's. These results support other studies that similarly concluded that limited technological infrastructure is one of the greatest challenges preventing the effective use of e-learning in Saudi Arabia (Alebaikan & Troudi, 2010; Al-Shehri, 2010; Gamdi & Samarji, 2016; Hussein, 2011). These previous results likely reflect the fact that the Internet was implemented in Saudi Arabia quite late by comparison with other countries (c.1999), due to governmental concerns and reservations at the time (Alshahrani, 2016). Even today there are only three telecommunications companies in the Saudi Arabian mobile market: STC, Mobily, and Zain (Alshahrani, 2016). However, the present study revealed that providing high-speed Internet connectivity with lower cost for students and technical support is a requirement in moving toward e-learning, consistent with findings by Alebaikan and Troudi (2010) who emphasized the need of Internet services sufficient to support e-learning. Similarly, the availability of reliable electricity was viewed as a key motivating factor in e-learning. Research by Alrashidi and Yahya (2014) also points toward the government's responsibility in providing electricity for the rural communities to effectively benefit from e-learning.

Furthermore, restrictive laws or policies were perceived to be large challenges to e-learning in Saudi Arabia, to the extent that these might prevent PNU and other universities from supporting e-learning at all. The study reported the need to enact appropriate policies favoring e-learning and raising awareness about the value of e-learning at both governmental and personal levels across the society. This present result supports Gamdi and Samarji's (2016) study, which concluded that the funding-strategic policies are required to support and expand the adoption of e-learning at Saudi universities. However, Al-Zahrani (2015b) reported a clear gap between strong policies that support e-learning and the lack of technology implementation present in Saudi Arabia. Through the narrative responses of the study, it was found that online learning and distance education are not accredited in the same manner as that of "traditional" education in Saudi Arabia, particularly in regards to recognition of these degrees within the job market. This, in turn, limits the enrollment of such programs. It is therefore apparent that the accreditation of higher education e-learning programs must carry the same perceived quality and prestige as traditional degrees by the job market if students are to be motivated to opt to study via e-learning.

The study also uncovered other perceived challenges, including concerns about the quality of the online courses; lack of awareness of the importance of e-learning; and lack of cooperation between universities in terms of the exchange of e-learning experiences. Regarding the quality of online learning, Ward, Peters, and Shelley (2010) asserted that the quality of learning achieved by students in a face-to-face environment can be achieved in an e-learning format. Educators who have worked extensively in online education know that e-learning can meet the same standards as traditional education, but this perception must find its way into the broad audience of students and faculty in Saudi Arabia if barriers to e-learning are to be overcome.

Limitations of the Study

The primary limitation of this study is that it was conducted at a single university in Saudi Arabia (PNU), rather than across multiple institutions. Additionally, although the $n = 306$ number is high in comparison to many educational research studies, this number reflects only a small segment of the target audience. It must also be noted that the collected data consists entirely of self-reporting. Whether or not participants felt fully comfortable in reporting their feelings and attitudes, or were accurate judges of the questions asked, is always an issue with self-reporting. Any limitations affect generalizability, but the number of participants in this study provides a relatively strong level of confidence in the study's generalizability to other similar institutions in Saudi Arabia and, potentially, to other countries with similar cultural settings.

Recommendations for Practice

We make the following recommendations regarding the use of e-learning in the Saudi higher education setting based on data collected from this study:

1. e-learning courses should be more commonly offered for Saudi higher education students to provide more flexible learning opportunities.
2. Accreditation of e-learning programs should be present, and should represent equivalent accomplishment to traditional settings via implementation of high quality e-learning curricula.
3. The technological infrastructure and technical support required to support e-learning learning must be implemented and/or strengthened at Saudi higher education institutions.
4. The current closed-circuit television modality used when male faculty members teach female students should be phased out over time and replaced with LMS-based systems to provide a richer and more interactive learning experience for female students.
5. Computer laboratories with high-speed Internet access should be made available to students at higher education institutions to accommodate those who may not have computers and/or Internet access at their homes.
6. Professional training programs that focus on the optimal use of technology in teaching should be mandated to help ensure

that instructors build the necessary technology skills for successful e-learning in Saudi universities.

Recommendations/Implications for Further Study

Despite previous studies that have been conducted on the topic of e-learning in Saudi Arabian higher education, very few studies have focused on the benefits of e-learning for Saudi female students. Few or none of these studies have been conducted on the differential benefits of e-learning course delivery for female students who are currently taught by male instructors using closed-circuit television. The current study may serve as a basis for future studies in further examining the effectiveness of e-learning-based course delivery when male instructors are teaching and interacting with female students. Insufficient information, too, is present concerning the perceptions of faculty and students on the effectiveness of online courses for Saudi female students, and so additional in-depth research using qualitative methods should be conducted to provide more insightful data in this area.

As this study was conducted at a single, female-only university in Saudi Arabia, it is also recommended that future research replicate this study in other female campuses at one or more Saudi universities to gather additional evidence concerning online course delivery for female students taught by male instructors. These studies can collect further important data revealing the views of female students and male instructors who teach in female campus about the suitability and effectiveness of online course delivery for this special educational in Saudi universities.

CONCLUSION

Universities worldwide have taken advantage of the benefits of e-learning by offering at least some coursework online, but many universities in Saudi Arabia are still reluctant to offer online courses. This reflects the limited experiences of e-learning among students and faculty members at Saudi universities. Consequently, there is an urgent need to actively and reflectively consider a new e-learning in Saudi higher education, particularly for the special situation when female students are taught by male instructors.

Although the setting on which this study focused is culturally unique (the case of male faculty members teaching female students), the vast bulk of what is already empirically known about e-learning will apply to this special case. Like many other countries that have already undergone this shift in educational delivery, Saudi Arabian universities will face a variety of challenges while undergoing this alteration in how its students are taught. The sheer number of students in Saudi Arabia who wish to achieve the highest levels of education, coupled with the limited number of in-person seats available to students in Saudi Arabia, make this transformation an imperative for the Kingdom. Understanding and addressing the challenges to e-learning in higher education is mandatory if Saudi Arabia is to proceed with successful e-learning adoption.

COMPLIANCE WITH ETHICAL STANDARDS

This study has no funding. The authors declare that they have no conflict of interest. All procedures performed in this study that involved human participants were in accordance with the ethical standards of the institutional and national research committee and with the 1964 Helsinki Declaration and its later amendments or comparable ethical standards. Informed consent was obtained from all individual participants included in the study.

REFERENCES

Akaslan, D., & Law, E. L. (2011, April). Measuring teachers' readiness for e-learning in higher education institutions associated with the subject of electricity in Turkey. In *Global Engineering Education Conference (EDUCON), 2011 IEEE* (pp. 481–490). New York, NY: IEEE.

Alahmari, A. (2017). The state of distance education in Saudi Arabia. *Quarterly Review of Distance Education, 18*(2), 91–98.

Alahmari, A., & Kyei-Blankson, L. (2016). Adopting and implementing an e-learning system for teaching and learning in Saudi public K–12 schools: The benefits, challenges, and concerns. *World Journal of Educational Research, 3*(1), 11–32. doi:10.22158/wjer.v3n1p11

Alamri, M. (2011). Higher education in Saudi Arabia. *Journal of Higher Education Theory and Practice, 11*(4), 88–91.

Al-Asmari, A. M., & Khan, M. R. (2014). E-learning in Saudi Arabia: Past, present and future. *Near & Middle Eastern Journal of Research in Education, 2*(1), 1–11. doi:10.5339/nmejre .2014.2

Alebaikan, R., & Troudi, S. (2010). Blended learning in Saudi universities: Challenges and perspectives. *Research in Learning Technology, 18*(1), 49–59

Al-Fahad, F. (2009). Students' attitudes and perceptions towards the effectiveness of mobile learning in King Saud University, Saudi Arabia. *Turkish Online Journal of Educational Technology, 8*(2), 111–119.

Alfahad, F. N. (2012). Effectiveness of using information technology in higher education in Saudi Arabia. *Procedia-Social and Behavioral Sciences, 46*, 1268–1278. doi:10.1016/j.sbspro .2012.05.287

Algarni, F., & Male, T. (2014). Leadership in Saudi Arabian public schools: Time for devolution? *International Studies In Educational Administration (Commonwealth Council For Educational Administration & Management (CCEAM)), 42*(3), 19–33.

Al-Hattami, A. A., Muammar, O. M., & Elmahdi, I. A. (2013). The need for professional training programs to improve faculty members teaching skills. *International Association of Social Science Research, 1*(2), 39–45

Aljabre, A. (2012). An exploration of distance learning in Saudi Arabian universities: Current practices and future possibilities. *International Journal of Business, Humanities and Technology, 2*(2), 132–137.

Allen, I. E., & Seaman, J. (2015). *Grade level: Tracking online education in the United States.*

Babson Survey Research Group and Quahog Research Group. Retrieved from http://www.onlinelearningsurvey.com/reports/gradelevel.pdf

Al Mousa, A. A. (2010). Experience of scholarships to foreign universities in Saudi Arabia: A model for investment in human resources & their contribution to development. In L. Bechir (Ed.), Arab Regional Conference on Higher Education (Cairo, May 31, June 1–2 2009). *Towards an Arab Higher Education Space: International Challenges and Societal Responsibilities* (pp. 717–724). Beirut, Lebanon: UNESCO Regional Bureau for Education in the Arab States.

Almutairy, S., Davies, T., & Dimitriadi, Y. (2015). The readiness of applying m-learning among Saudi Arabian students at higher education. *International Journal of Interactive Mobile Technologies*, *9*(3), 33–36. doi:10.3991/ijim.v9i3.4423

Al-Seghayer, K. (2011). *English teaching in Saudi Arabia: Status, issues, and challenges*. Riyadh, Saudi Arabia: Hala.

Alshahrani, H. A. (2016). A brief history of the Internet in Saudi Arabia. *TechTrends*, *60*(1), 19–20. doi:10.1016/s0308-5961(01)00036-2

Alshangeeti, A., Alsaghier, H., & Nguyen, A. (2009). Faculty perceptions of attributes affecting the diffusion of online learning in Saudi Arabia: A quantitative study. In *Proceedings of the 4th International Conference on E-Learning* (pp. 10–24), University of Toronto, Canada, July 16–17.

Al-Shehri, A. M. (2010). E-learning in Saudi Arabia: "To E or not to E, that is the question." *Journal of Family & Community Medicine*, *17*(3), 147–150. doi:10.4103/1319 1683.74333

Alrashidi, A., & Yahya N. (2014). E-learning in Saudi Arabia: A review of the literature. *British Journal of Education, Society & Behavioral Science*, *4*(5), 656–672.

Altameem, T. (2011). Contextual mobile learning system for Saudi Arabian universities. *International Journal of Computer Applications*, *21*(4), 21–26.

Alturise, F. (2013). Benefits and challenges of using ICT in Saudi Arabia universities: A literature review. *International Journal of Information Technology & Computer Science*, *11*(2), 46–57.

Al-Zahrani, A. M. (2015a). Enriching professional practice with digital technologies: Faculty performance indicators and training needs in Saudi higher education. *International Journal of Instructional Technology and Distance Learning*, *12*(1), 44–57.

Al-Zahrani, A. M. (2015b). Faculty satisfaction with online teaching in Saudi Arabia's higher education institutions. *International Journal of Instructional Technology and Distance Learning*, *12*(4), 17–28.

Asiri, H. A. (2014). Challenges of the health informatics education in the Kingdom of Saudi Arabia: What stands in our way? *Journal of Health Informatics in Developing Countries*, *8*(1), 26–35.

Asiri, M. J., bt Mahmud, R., Bakar, K. A., & bin Mohd Ayub, A. F. (2012). Factors influencing the use of learning management system in Saudi Arabian higher education: A theoretical framework. *Higher Education Studies*, *2*(2), 125–137.

Baqutayan, S. (2011). Issues in the implementation of science and technology education in Saudi Arabia. *International Journal of Psychological Studies, 1*(5), 165–170

Bousbahi, F., & Alrazgan, M. S. (2015). Investigating IT faculty resistance to learning management system adoption using latent variables in an acceptance technology model. *The Scientific World Journal, 2015*, 1–11.

El Zawaidy, H. (2014). Using Blackboard in online learning at Saudi universities: Faculty member's perceptions and existing obstacles. *International Interdisciplinary Journal of Education, 3*(7), 145–154.

Gamdi, M. A. A., & Samarji, A. (2016). Perceived barriers towards e-learning by faculty members at a recently established university in Saudi Arabia. *International Journal of Information and Education Technology, 6*(1), 23–28. doi:10.7763/ijiet.2016.v6.652

Green, S., & Salkind, N. (2014). *Using SPSS for Windows and Macintosh: Analyzing and understanding data* (7th ed.). Boston, MA: Prentice Hall.

Holden, H., & Rada, R. (2011). Understanding the influence of perceived usability and technology self-efficacy on teachers' technology acceptance. *Journal of Research on Technology in Education, 43*(4), 343–367. doi:10.1080/15391523.2011.10782576

Human Development Reports. (2013). Expenditure on education, Public (% of GDP) (%). Retrieved from http://hdr.undp.org/en/content/expenditure-education-public-gdp

Hussein, H. B. (2011). Attitudes of Saudi universities faculty members towards using learning management system (JUSUR). *Turkish Online Journal of Educational Technology, 10*(2), 43–53.

Jabli, N., & Qahmash, A. (2013). The benefits and barriers of e-learning in higher education in Saudi Arabia. *Journal of Emerging Trends in Computing and Information Sciences, 4*(11), 877–880.

Lee, L. (2016). Autonomous learning through task-based instruction in fully online language courses. *Language Learning & Technology, 20*(2), 81–97.

MacWilliams, B. (2000). Turkey's old-fashioned distance education draws the largest student body on earth. *Chronicle of Higher Education, 47*(4), 41–42.

Matthews, D. (1999). The origins of distance education. *THE. Journal, 27*(2), 56–66.

Ministry of Education. (2015). Higher education statistics 2014–2015. Retrieved from https://www.moe.gov.sa/ar/Ministry/Deputy-Ministry-for-Planning-and-Information-affairs/HESC/Ehsaat/Pages/default.aspx

Mirza A. A. (2007). Utilizing distance learning technologies to deliver courses in a segregated educational environment. In *Proceedings of EdMedia: World Conference on Educational Multimedia, Hypermedia and Telecommunications* (pp. 126–129). Waynesville, NC: Association for the Advancement of Computing in Education.

Mirza, A., & Al-Abdulkareem, M. (2011). Models of e-learning adopted in the Middle East. *Applied Computing and Informatics, 9*(2), 83–93.

Mohsen, T., & Reg, D. (2011). Making sense of Cronbach's alpha. *International Journal of Medical Education, 2*(1), 53–55.

Mosa, A. A., Naz'ri bin Mahrin, M., & Ibrahim, R. (2016). Technological aspects of e-learning readiness in higher education: A review of the literature. *Computer and Information Science, 9*(1), 113–127.

OPEC. (2016). Saudi Arabia Facts and Figures. Retrieved from http://www.opec.org/opec_web/en/about_us/169.htm

Ouma, G. O., Awuor, F. M., & Kyambo, B. (2013). Evaluation of e-learning readiness in secondary schools in Kenya. *World Applied Programming Journal, 3*(10), 493–503.

Pavan, A. (2013). A new perspective on the quest for education: The Saudi Arabian way to knowledge society. *Higher Education Studies, 3*(6), 25–34.

Roberts, C. M. (2010). *The dissertation journey: A practical and comprehensive guide to planning, writing, and defending your dissertation.* Thousand Oaks, CA: Corwin.

Simonson, M., Smaldino, S., Albright, M., & Zvacek, S. (2014). *Teaching and learning at a distance: Foundations of distance education* (6th ed.) Charlotte, NC: Information Age.

Taylor, C., & Albasri, W. (2014). The impact of Saudi Arabia King Abdullah's scholarship program in the US. *Open Journal of Social Sciences, 2*(10), 109–118.

U.S.-Saudi Arabian Business Council. (2015). Saudi Arabia's 2015 budget maintains strong spending, diversification initiatives. Retrieved from https://www.ussabc.org/custom/news/details.cfm?id=1645

van Geel, A. (2016). Separate or together? Women-only public spaces and participation of Saudi women in the public domain in Saudi Arabia. *Contemporary Islam*, 1–22. doi:10.1007/s11562-015-0350-2

Ward, M. E., Peters, G., & Shelley, K. (2010). Student and faculty perceptions of the quality of online learning experiences. *International Review of Research in Open & Distance Learning, 11*(3), 57–77.

Weber, A. S. (2009). E-learning in the Gulf Cooperation Council Countries (GCC): Problems and prospects. In V. Uskov (Ed.), *Proceedings of Web-Based Education 2009* (pp. 95–100), Phuket, Thailand, March 16-18. London, England: Acta

Yamin, M. (2015). A socio-cultural overview of e-learning in Saudi Arabia. *International Women Online Journal of Distance Education, 4*(3), 72–77.

PSYCHOMOTOR SKILLS, PHYSICAL THERAPY, AND A HYBRID COURSE
A Case Study

Melissa J. Lazinski
Nova Southeastern University

INTRODUCTION

Approximately 75% of the content of a typical doctor of physical therapy (PT) course does not require the instructor and students to be together in the same classroom, laboratory, or clinic. Physical therapist education includes a large amount of psychomotor clinical skills. Traditionally, psychomotor skills are taught face to face in laboratory courses with teacher-led skill introduction and demonstration followed by student practice with instructor feedback (Gaida et al., 2016; Maloney, Storr, Paynter, Morgan, & Ilic, 2013). A goal of hybrid course redesign is to balance elements essential to face to face with those that can be delivered online. Ideally, online and face-to-face classrooms work in a symbiotic way without being duplicative. The dynamic nature of learning psychomotor skills makes hybrid redesign of PT courses challenging. This article describes the redesign of a traditional PT lab course using the community of inquiry (CoI) model as a framework and Google Blogger as the main platform for an online skills lab. A description and discussion of course design, time allocations, student learning outcomes, and student perceptions are provided.

Student needs for flexibility and rising health care workforce demands influence a trend toward hybrid delivery in health care education; however, substantiation of the ways technology can effectively replace face-to-face instruction is needed (Brandt, Quake-Rapp, Shanedling, Spannaus-Martin, & Martin, 2010). Hybrid education is a category of distance education in which online activities replace face-to-face activities. This contrasts with other models of blended learning such as a *flipped* classroom, which incorporate online instruction as an adjunct to face-to-face instruction without a reduction of face-to-face time. Garrison and Vaughn (2008) described hybrid or blended learning as a "thoughtful fusion of face-to-face and online learning experiences" (p. 8). The CoI model provides a

• **Melissa Lazinski**, Associate Professor, Physical Therapy, Dr. Pallavi Patel College of Health Care Sciences, Nova Southeastern University. Telephone: (813) 574-5313. E-mail: mj.lazinski@nova.edu

The Quarterly Review of Distance Education, Volume 18(4), 2017, pp. 57–69   ISSN 1528-3518

framework for hybrid course design using online and face-to-face instruction in a way that each mode enhances without duplicating the other (Garrison, Anderson, & Archer, 2010). The mixture of online and face-to-face activities varies from case to case (Means et al., 2013). In the CoI model, three essential components overlap to create an educational experience: *teaching presence, cognitive presence*, and *social presence* (Garrison & Vaughn, 2008; see Figure 1). Teaching presence is the design of class activities, facilitation of discourse, and direction of instruction. Cognitive presence comes as students engage, explore, and integrate the course content. Social presence occurs as class participants interact in open communication, to build camaraderie and group cohesion (Garrison & Vaughn, 2008).

Educational Technology in Physical Therapy Education

Recent systematic reviews found that integration of educational technologies in health care education was equivalent or better than

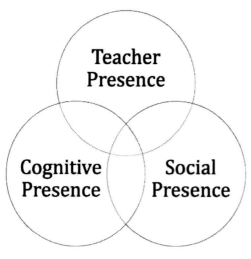

Source: Garrison and Vaughn (2008).

FIGURE 1
Community of inquiry model

traditional teaching methods alone (George et al., 2014; Rasmussen et al., 2014). Heterogeneity of studies prevents more definitive conclusions, but emerging evidence supports the use of educational technologies in PT education. A variety of approaches have been described including flipped classroom methods, using supplemental technology resources, and using collaborative technology tools. As in higher education in general, PT education most commonly uses technology to teach didactic content or achieve cognitive objectives (Rowe, Bozalek, & Frantz, 2013). In studies comparing a flipped model to traditional teaching methods for didactic content, student learning outcomes and perceptions varied, but variation in methods may account for some of the differences. One study found improved student learning outcomes using flipped methods (Boucher, Robertson, Wainner, & Sanders, 2013). Another found no difference in overall student performance scores, but those in the flipped group did better with higher order questions (Bayliss & Warden, 2011). A third found no difference in student achievement between traditional and flipped methods (Murray, McCallum, & Petrosino, 2014). In this case, students were provided previewing materials, but face-to-face class times began with 20–30 minute lectures, which may have undermined the need for preparation, an important component of the flipped model. Student perceptions were positive for previewing prerecorded lectures before class (Boucher et al., 2013), but showed no increased preference for previewing Power-Point lecture slides (not recordings) (Bayliss & Warden, 2011). The variety of techniques used make it difficult to draw global conclusions.

Supplemental online or computer activities in addition to traditional instruction have shown favorable results in cognitive learning outcomes and student perceptions, in higher education in general (Cain & Pitre, 2008; Meyer, 2014). In a neurological PT course, it was found that students with access to supplemental computer modules with embedded video and practice questions had better clinical reasoning and learning outcomes compared to receiving traditional lecture and lab alone (Veneri & Gannotti, 2014). In addition, student perceptions of learning were better in the group with the added computer modules. Similarly, Gardner et al., (2016) investigated student perceptions of an e-learning package to teach PT students about rheumatoid arthritis. The e-learning package was given in addition to three live lectures about general chronic disease management. Students had positive perceptions of the experience and preferred a blended approach to the subject matter. Rowe and colleagues (2013) used Google Drive as a platform for a blended PT case activity and found that students valued the authentic learning approach and had shifts in their perceptions about learning. In an online PT pharmacology course that incorporated a collaborative learning activity, students had positive attitudes about the course design without a change in the grade distribution (Pittenger & Olson-Kellogg, 2012).

Teaching psychomotor skills with educational technologies and blended methods has emerging support in the literature, but like didactic content there are a variety of methods and outcomes reported. Some studies found no difference in outcomes between traditional and methods using technology (Maloney, Storr, Paynter, et al., 2013; VanDuijn, Swanick, & Donald, 2014), and others found improved outcomes with the use of technology (Arroyo-Morales et al., 2012; Maloney, Storr, Morgan, & Ilic, 2013; Preston et al., 2012). Physical therapy students have reported higher perceived satisfaction with blended methods of teaching psychomotor skills, particularly including video versus traditional methods (Coffee & Hillier, 2008; Gaida et al., 2016; Hurst, 2016; Maloney, Storr, Morgan, et al. 2013; Maloney, Storr, Paynter, et al., 2013). Video has been show to enhance engagement, social presence, and learning (Kliger & Pfeiffer, 2011). Further, incorporating student-produced skill demonstration videos (self-videos) were found to improve student skill performance on assessments and increase

students' perceptions of educational value over traditional teaching methods (Maloney, Storr, Morgan, et al., 2013; Maloney, Storr, Paynter, et al., 2013).

Regardless of approach, mastering psychomotor skills requires instructor presence through feedback. Traditionally this occurs in the classroom setting face-to-face (Gaida et al., 2016); however, video can be used as a vehicle for receiving feedback at a distance. Student self-videos of skill performance have been effectively used to give formative feedback on performance at a distance (Maloney, Storr, Morgan, et al., 2013; Maloney, Storr, Paynter, et al., 2013).

Available studies investigating the use of blended models or supplemental education technologies in PT education have studied learning outcomes, student perceptions, and satisfaction with favorable findings. No study could be found that investigated changes in the distribution of time as an outcome. This is an important consideration in the implementation of a hybrid course design in which face-to-face time is replaced by online time, because the shift in time allocation has implications for students and faculty. In addition, heterogeneity of studied instructional methods makes findings difficult to interpret (George et al., 2014; Rasmussen et al., 2014; Veneri, 2011). Evidence is lacking for teaching psychomotor skills in a hybrid course whereby online instruction replaces traditional face-to-face instruction.

Case Description

The course was a 1-credit hour laboratory course focused on psychomotor and affective objectives of performing surface palpation. It was part of the first-year curriculum of the Nova Southeastern University Hybrid Doctor of Physical Therapy Program (HDPT). The course was converted to hybrid from an existing traditional course that met weekly. The redesigned hybrid course occurred in a 16-week semester with four face-to-face on-campus institutes. Four-day on-campus institutes took place throughout the semester at the end of every fourth week (Thursday through Sunday). The class met for a 3-hour face-to-face lab session at each on-campus institute for a total of 12 face-to-face instructional hours. This equates to 25% of the face-to-face time if the course was taught traditionally (completely face to face), with the remainder of class-time (75%) occurring online.

Initial course redesign began by differentiating activities that must occur face-to-face from those that could occur online. The conclusion was that two key components must occur face to face: (a) face-to-face practice with feedback and (b) skills assessment. Given the on-campus institute time constraints, it was decided students should have an introduction and be practicing skills online in preparation for face-to-face time. The layout of the course schedule placed one body region in each week for 12 weeks, with 4 weeks remaining at the end of the course for review of cardinal plane

joint motions and application of palpated landmarks to postural assessment.

The course design was constructed with components that created the elements of the CoI model (see Figure 2). Activities that supported these design components were carefully selected with the underlying pedagogy in mind and the understanding that technology does not drive student achievement (Means, Toyama, Murphy, Bakia, & Jones, 2010; Meyer, 2014).

ONLINE CLASSROOM

Constrained face-to-face time required students to arrive to the physical classroom having been introduced to a skill set and having basic proficiency. To include instruction, deliberate practice, and feedback in a meaningful way during online time, instructor, cognitive, and social presence were considered in the online course design. Instructional content was delivered via textbook and video. A text

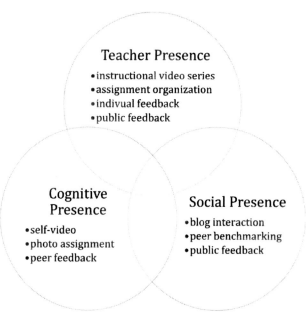

FIGURE 2
Community of Inquiry Model
Complete With Course Design Components

was selected for its format, engaging illustrations, and accompanying instructional DVD. Supplemental videos were produced by the course instructor and published online for content not adequately covered by the text-companion DVD.

Deliberate practice and feedback were incorporated in course design through weekly online assignments with the goal of moving beyond skill introduction and toward proficiency prior to on-campus institute. To reach proficiency with psychomotor skills requires feedback. Students took turns rotating through one of two assignments each week where they could receive feedback from instructor and classmates. For one assignment, students identified and labeled palpation landmarks on a partner volunteer, which they photographed and submitted to the instructor. They received private instructor feedback on landmark palpation accuracy.

A second, video-based assignment incorporated all components of the CoI model, most notably social presence. In it, students made short self-videos demonstrating palpation on a partner that was shared using a class weblog (blog). The class blog, hosted on Google Blogger, was private and restricted to members of the course. An outside blog platform was chosen for ease of use, especially for embedding video, as compared to the university learning management system. In addition, the class blog remained available as a resource to students after the course ended. The entire class had authorship allowing them to post and comment freely. Classmates were required to watch each other's videos and give feedback comments to one classmate weekly. Peer coaching has been found to improve psychomotor skill development in nursing students (Himes & Ravert, 2012). An instructor gave feedback comments to all videos using a feedback guideline that included dimensions of communication, positioning, body mechanics, draping, technique, accuracy, and time management. All posts and feedback comments (students' and instructor's) were visible to all members of the class blog.

A shared blog allows collaborative online learning between presenter and audience, enhances social presence, and can positively affect student learning (De Jong, Savin-Baden, Cunningham, & Verstegen, 2014; Fluckiger, Vigil, Pasco, & Danielson, 2010; Huang, Huang, & Yu, 2011; Means et al., 2013; Tan, Ladyshewsky, & Gardner, 2010). Blogs also overcome some face-to-face classroom limitations like space shortages, time constraints, and student anxiety about evaluating peer work (Huang et al., 2011). Student-class-instructor interaction in the class blog also allows peer benchmarking that can improve student self-assessment and understanding of performance expectations (Maloney, Storr, Paynter, et al., 2013).

Face-to-Face Classroom

With all skills introduced and practiced online, face-to-face lab time was used for refinement and mastery of palpation skills in preparation for practical skills assessment. During a 3-hour lab session, students rotated through stations supervised by lab instructors who reviewed content and gave hands-on feedback. An optional, unstructured practice time was available to students outside of class with a lab assistant present to answer questions.

Each on-campus institute ended with a practical skills assessment of psychomotor learning. performance dimensions, as in the video assignment, were proper techniques, body mechanics, positioning, draping, accuracy, communication, and time management. The fourth and final skills check was cumulative.

OUTCOMES

Subjects were 123 first-year DPT students (71 females) from three successive cohorts spanning 2012-2014 (cohorts A, B, C respectively). Outcomes were analyzed including (a) student performance scores on practical skills assessments, (b) online engagement rates, and (c)

TABLE 1
Blog Engagement

	Cohort		
Engagement With Blog	A (n = 39)	B (n = 39)	C (n = 45)
Page views per student per week	10	8.3	10.1
Original post rate for cohort (percent of required)	100%	98%	99%
Commenting rate for cohort (percent of required)	182%	199%	186%

Note: Engagement values based on actual counts obtained from blog corrected for instructor activity. Engagement rates reported as a percentage of actual activity as compared to expected activity based on assignment instructions/requirements.

student course evaluations. Performance scores and engagement rates were analyzed using descriptive statistics. Course evaluation rating scores were analyzed using descriptive statistics and comments were thematically analyzed. One subject of the 2014 cohort withdrew from the university at the beginning of the course and these data were removed from analysis.

Online Participation and Engagement

As a measure of student engagement in the online lab activity, counts of student blog page views, blog posts, and comments were collected from the blog statistics page. Students met posting requirements with few exceptions. Students exceeded the required/expected number of peer comments and page views at a rate of roughly double the comments and 8–10 times the page views (see Table 1).

STUDENT PERFORMANCE

Practical skills assessments required that students perform palpation skills on a preselected set of palpation landmarks drawn at random. Performance was scored using a score sheet that captured performance dimension like those of the video assignment on a binary met/not-met scale. The score sheet was created by the lead faculty, a physical therapist, who was board certified in orthopedic physical therapy

and a certified clinical instructor. It was used in its original form with a preceding cohort and refined with input from other faculty subject matter experts. While no formal validity testing was performed, the development process gives the score sheet increased face and construct validity. To improve score reliability, it was standard practice for course faculty to meet after testing and to reach consensus on any points of concern or disagreement in grading. Seventy-five was set as a passing score as per HDPT program policy. The range of median performance scores was high but narrow (see Table 2). Among the three cohorts, only one failing score on a skills check was recorded.

Course Evaluations and Student Perceptions

Online course evaluation surveys were completed anonymously online. The response rate was 100% as it is a university requirement. The survey contained space for open commenting and six scored sections: course organization, course activities, grading, preparation of course material, delivery of instruction, and student-instructor interactions. Each section contained 5–7 items ranked on a 4-point Likert scale (1 = *strongly disagree* to 4 = *strongly agree*). Sections with items that most related to the CoI model included course organization, preparation of course material, course activities, and student-instructor interaction. Survey

TABLE 2
Student Performance on Skills Assessments

Student Performance (%)	Cohort		
	A (n = 39)	B (n = 39)	C (n = 45)
Skill Assessment 1	98.00 (88–100)	86.00 (65–91)	86.00 (74–91)
Skill Assessment 2	98.00 (89–100)	93.50 (78–100)	96.00 (82–100)
Skill Assessment 3	98.00 (91–100)	95.00 (87–100)	97.00 (89–99)
Skill Assessment 4 (cumulative)	96.67 (91–100)	95.79 (78–99)	96.97 (81–99)
Final Course Grade	97.85 (93–100)	91.53 (78–94)	96.50 (91–99)

Note: Student performance score reported as median (range).

TABLE 3
Course Evaluation Section Scores

Course Evaluation Section	Cohort			3-Year Mean
	A (n = 39)	B (n = 39)	C (n = 45)	
Course Organization	3.64, 0.84	3.83, 0.58	3.57. 0.86	3.68
Course Activities	3.69, 0.73	3.84, 0.54	3.58, 0.80	3.70
Grading	3.68, 0.73	3.80, 0.56	3.56, 0.82	3.68
Preparation of Course Material	3.80, 0.56	3.93, 0.25	3.64, 0.79	3.79
Delivery of Instruction	3.77, 0.58	3.89, 0.31	3.62, 0.80	3.76
Student-Instructor Interaction	3.76, 0.58	3.89, 0.25	3.62, 0.79	3.76
Overall mean score				

Note: Section items ranked on a 4-point Likert Scale: 1 = *strongly disagree*; 2 = *disagree*; 3 = *agree*; 4 = *strongly agree*. Section values reported as mean, standard deviation.

items mostly pertained to instructor presence and were completely lacking in items pertaining to social presence. Rankings in all sections were consistently high over the 3-year period. Mean section rankings ranged from 3.56–3.93 and median score for all sections was 4.0 (see Table 3).

Students gave feedback in two open comment sections on the course evaluations pertaining to the overall course and to the lead instructor. One hundred and five comments were reviewed and thematically coded (see Table 4). Six themes emerged from the comments: student satisfaction/engagement, teaching presence—course design, teaching presence—responsiveness, cognitive pres-

ence, social presence, and assessment. The most common comments pertained to satisfaction/engagement with the course and included descriptors such as, "fun," "excellent," "enjoyed," and "favorite."

Comments in the teaching presence—course design theme referred to being well organized, having clear expectations, aiding time management, and instruction (see Table 4). The comments were generally positive. One student wrote "I felt like I knew what was expected of me ahead of time, and I had ample time to prepare." Another wrote, "there were no surprises." Another commented that he/she "felt prepared for … institute and institute felt more like a review." Some constructive feed-

TABLE 4
Course Evaluation Comment Themes

Themes	Descriptors (Comment Count)
Satisfaction/engagement	General positive comments (33)
Teaching presence–course design	Organization, expectations, time management, instruction (33)
Teaching presence—responsiveness	Feedback and face-to-face interaction (21)
Cognitive presence	Learning, hands-on practice, and course assignments (24)
Social presence	Peer interaction and peer benchmarking (5)
Assessment	Grader consistency and fairness (5)

Note: Major themes with comment descriptors from analysis of comments of three successive cohorts.

back was given regarding videos and face-to-face time. One student suggested that videos be more detailed and descriptive, and another suggested more instructor-made videos, versus the text companion DVD. While comments were largely positive regarding face-to-face instruction, four students felt that the time was too short and one felt it was too long.

Teaching presence—responsiveness theme comments related to feedback and face-to-face interaction. Comments about both formative and summative feedback online and face-to-face were very common and largely positive (see Table 4). Some students also commented positively on the timeliness of feedback, highlighting the temporal quality of this theme. Further, students commented about a period when feedback was unavailable due to a technical problem. Some gave constructive feedback in this theme pertaining to perceived variability between online instruction (text and video), face-to-face instruction (in lab), and between individual lab assistants in lab.

The cognitive presence theme emerged with comments related to learning, hands-on practice, and course assignments (see Table 4). Comments in this theme support positive student learning perceptions in both online and face-to-face modes. Some commented that assignments and varied media enhanced learning, with one student noting a preference for video over photo assignments and another writing that "the video blog is a great idea." One student commented that he or she

"learned the most in class on institute weekends"; however, three students referred to "hands-on" learning as a positive aspect of the course despite being largely taught online at a distance. This paradox is underscored by the comment "never knew that I can [sic] learn palpation online!"

Social presence was not measured in the course evaluation survey, but was evident in student comments. While not as prevalent, comments about peer interaction and peer benchmarking emerged as a social presence theme (see Table 4). Several students commented positively on the use of videos and a blog as an assignment platform that allowed for interaction. One student commented "I liked having the opportunity to get feedback from … classmates on a weekly basis." Another student reflected peer benchmarking in the comment, "I really like being able to see what my classmates are doing in their videos." No constructive feedback was given in this theme area, except the feedback that video assignments were preferred to photo assignments. It is not known if the lack of social presence survey items affected contributed to the lack of open comments offered.

The final theme, assessments, emerged in comments about course assessments and their scoring (see Table 4). These comments were split. Two students commented that assessments were "fair," while three students commented on perceived inconsistencies between graders. These three comments came only from cohort B, but are consistent with comments about variation between instructors in the face-to-face lab.

DISCUSSION AND CONCLUSION

It is common perception that psychomotor physical therapy skills must be learned with the instructor and students working together in the same lab, classroom, or clinic. Rather, 75% of the instruction in a psychomotor physical therapy course was successfully taught to distant learners challenging the notion that while educational technologies are effective supplements to traditional teaching, they could not be a replacement for them (Arroyo-Morales et al., 2012; Davies, Ramsay, Lindfield, & Couperthwaite, 2005). While technologies have demonstrated benefit to student learning outcomes and student perceptions, their ability to replace face-to-face class time has not been a focus in PT education research. This case report describes the hybrid redesign of a traditional course using the CoI model. The outcomes demonstrate a significant savings in face-to-face instructional time with favorable learning outcomes and student satisfaction.

Students generally have positive perceptions of using educational technology and blended approaches. Accessibility, flexibility, and time to reflect and prepare are positive features of the hybrid course design (Garrison & Vaughn, 2008). In a hybrid course, promoting student engagement online is an important factor because of competing time and attention demands outside a physical classroom and fewer ways to connect when at a distance (Meyer, 2014). Tools such as blogs, that facilitate and enhance student-teacher interaction, establish social presence, which improves outcomes and empower students in their learning (Kliger & Pfeiffer, 2011; Means, Toyama, Murphy, Bakia, & Jones, 2010; Rowe, Bozalek, & Frantz, 2013). In this case, a course blog served as a virtual meeting place to reduce social and psychological distance between course members, which is a positive predictor

of student perception of learning and satisfaction (Meyer, 2014).

There were limited constructive or negative comments received across three cohorts of feedback. What was received related to instructional variations between instructors face-to-face, between feedback online versus face-to-face, or between graders during assessments. Attempts were made proactively to standardize instructed skills; however, there exists technique variation among physical therapists, often with several correct ways to perform a skill. These student comments may be a function of the novice learner not yet comfortable reconciling this variability. More thorough qualitative methodology such as focus groups may be better suited to generate constructive feedback in future research.

In contrast to other studies, technology was not found to be a detractor, barrier, or consideration for participants in this course (Button, Harrington, & Belan, 2014; Dejong et al., 2014; Hayward, 2004; Kliger & Pfeiffer, 2011). In this case, the sample was comprised of students enrolled in a program delivered entirely in hybrid format. As such, participants have an expectation of heavy technology use and may be more technology literate and tolerant.

While student satisfaction and engagement is desirable, alone it gives limited insight into the achievement of desired learning outcomes. In the current study, student learning outcomes were favorable across three cohorts. Without a comparison group, it is impossible to assert superiority of any teaching method based on these results. In a systematic review with meta-analysis, hybrid education was found more effective than traditional or online-only education (Means et al., 2010). This may be because of the varied instructional techniques, expanded learning time, and space to practice and reflect that this delivery method affords (Garrison & Vaughn, 2008; Means et al., 2010). Course activities that included peer-to-peer feedback facilitate independence in learning (Ashgar, 2010; Bayliss & Warden, 2011; Himes & Ravert, 2012; Moore, Westwater-

Wood, & Kerry, 2016). Creating self-videos facilitates improved performance on assessments by promoting self-critique and reflection-on-action through attention to performance, behaviors, and mannerisms (Maloney, Storr, Morgan, et al., 2013; Maloney, Storr, Paynter, et al., 2013; Stephens & Parr, 2013).

The three elements of the CoI model used to design the course were evident in course feedback. In contrast to the basic three elements of the model, four themes emerged from student comments reflecting two subthemes of teacher presence: course design and responsiveness (Carlon et al., 2012). Course design relates to matters of organization, clear instruction, tool selection, and planning assignments that support student learning through sound pedagogical choices (Dejong et al., 2014; Meyer, 2014). Responsiveness, related to instructor behaviors and timeliness of communication, are positive predictors of student perceptions and improve outcomes (Kliger & Pfeiffer, 2011; Meyer, 2014).

Social presence was the weakest theme to emerge from student comments, but was evidenced by blog participation rates. It is noteworthy that the course feedback survey lacked items related to social presence, which may have contributed to its underrepresentation in the comments. Alternatively, perhaps components of the course design intended to create social presence were not sufficient or social connection in the online portion of the course is not a priority for this sample of students who see each other monthly. More in-depth investigation is needed to address this question, but the current research will be used to inform revisions to the course feedback survey to better evaluate social presence in future HDPT courses.

Analysis of faculty outcomes was not part of this case; however, faculty are a pivotal component of hybrid course delivery. The initial design of a hybrid course and online set-up requires considerable time, skill, and resources (Button et al., 2014; Pittinger & Olson-Kellogg, 2012; Rowe et al., 2013). Care must be taken to identify quality instructional materials or produce them when unavailable. Once established, faculty technology literacy, overarching support from administration, and technology support staff are potential barriers (Meyer, 2014; Phillips, Forbes, & Duke, 2013). While flexible, time demands are considerable and hybrid delivery may not decrease faculty time, but merely change when and how time is spent. In this case, time spent tending to the online course ranged from 5–6 hours per week (for a 1-credit hour lab course). More study is needed to realistically analyze the workload and resource demands of blended teaching models.

This case report has several limitations. The context of the described course is uniquely situated within a completely hybrid-delivered DPT program. This may limit generalizability and potentially introduces selection bias. Participant students, faculty, and administration involved have the expectation of heavy technology use and results may not be easily reproduced in another curricular context. Validity, reliability, and precision of the skill assessment instrument is not known and grader variation was one of the negative comments received from students. The grading instrument was created and tested in an iterative process by a team of content experts, which gives face and content validity at best. Attempts to improve reliability were made by training proctors to use the instrument, maintaining a consistent pool of graders across assessments, and conducting postassessment discussion to clarify and standardize scoring by consensus. Scoring subjectivity was reduced by scoring criteria based on a met/not-met scale, but this reduced measurement sensitivity and contributed to the low stratification of assessment grades.

More in-depth qualitative analysis including focus groups is needed to explore possible constructive feedback or negative perceptions. Further quantitative research is needed to compare outcomes of psychomotor objectives taught with hybrid versus traditional teaching methods to support the most effective and efficient teaching methods.

Despite the prevailing traditional model for the instruction of psychomotor skills, this case report suggests that hybrid delivery is capable of achieving satisfactory outcomes with a substantial reduction of face-to-face time. Purposeful course redesign using the CoI framework, sound pedagogical principles, and supportive technology that did not supersede pedagogy was used to create a rich online lab environment that complemented a face-to-face lab classroom.

Strategies described in this case report have been adopted and adapted for use in other courses in the HDPT program with psychomotor and affective skills.

Author Note: This article was also published in Volume 14, Issue 4 of *Distance Learning*.

REFERENCES

Arroyo-Morales, M., Cantarero-Villanueva, I., Fernández-Lao, C., Guirao-Piñeyro, M., Castro-Martín, E., & Díaz-Rodríguez, L. (2012). A blended learning approach to palpation and ultrasound imaging skills through supplementation of traditional classroom teaching with an e-learning package. *Manual Therapy, 17*(5), 474–478. https://doi.org/10.1016/j.math.2012.04.002

Asghar, A. M. (2010). Reciprocal peer coaching and its use as a formative assessment strategy for first-year students. *Assessment & Evaluation in Higher Education, 35*(4), 403–417. Retrieved from https://doi.org/10.1080/02602930902862834

Bayliss, A. J., & Warden, S. J. (2011). A hybrid model of student-centered instruction improved physical therapist student performance in cardiopulmonary practice patterns by enhancing performance in higher cognitive domains. *Journal of Physical Therapy Education, 25*(3), 14–20. Retrieved from http://www.aptaeducation.org/members/jopte/index.cfm

Boucher, B., Robertson, E., Wainner, R., & Sanders, B. (2013). "Flipping" Texas State University's physical therapist musculoskeletal

curriculum: Implementation of a hybrid learning model. *Journal of Physical Therapy Education, 27*(3), 72–77. Retrieved from http://www.aptaeducation.org/members/jopte/index.cfm

Brandt, B. F., Quake-Rapp, C., Shanedling, J., Spannaus-Martin, D., & Martin, P. (2010). Blended learning: Emerging best practices in allied health workforce development. *Journal of Allied Health, 39*(4), e167-e172. Retrieved from http://www.asahp.org/journal-of-allied-health/

Button, D., Harrington, A., & Belan, I. (2014). E-learning & information communication technology (ICT) in nursing education: A review of the literature. *Nurse Education Today, 34*(2014), 1311–1323. https://doi.org/10.1016/j.nedt.2013.05.002

Cain, D. L., & Pitre, P. E. (2008). The effect of computer mediated conferencing and computer assisted instruction on student learning outcomes. *Journal of Asynchronous Learning Networks, 12*(3–4), 31–52. Retrieved from https://secure.onlinelearningconsortium.org/publications/olj_main

Carlon, S., Bennett-Woods, D., Berg, B., Claywell, L., LeDuc, K, … Zenoni, L. (2012). The community of inquiry instrument: Validation and results in online health care disciplines. *Computers & Education, 59*(2012), 215–221. Retrieved from https://doi.org/10.1016/j.compedu.2012.01.004

Coffee, J. A., & Hillier, S. (2008). Teaching precursor clinical skills using an online audio-visual tool: An evaluation using student responses. *MERLOT Online Journal of Learning and Teaching, 4*(4), 8. Retrieved from http://jolt.merlot.org/vol4no4/coffee_1208.pdf

Davies A., Ramsay J., Lindfield, H., & Couperthwaite, J. (2005). A blended approach to learning: Added value and lessons learnt from students' use of computer-based materials for neurological analysis. *British Journal of Educational Technology, 35*(5), 839–849. https://doi.org/10.1111/j.1467-8535.2005.00506.x

De Jong, N., Savin-Baden, M., Cunningham, A. M., & Verstegen, D. M. L. (2014). Blended learning in health education: Three case studies. *Perspectives in Medical Education, 3*, 278–288. https://doi.org/10.0007/s40037-014-0108-1

Fluckiger, J., Vigil, Y. T., Pasco, R., & Danielson, K. (2010). Formative feedback: Involving students as partners in assessment to enhance learning. *College Teaching, 58*(4), 136–140. http://doi.org/10.1080/87567555.2010.484031

Gaida, J. J., Seville, C., Cope, L., Dalwood, N., Morgan, P., & Maloney, S. (2016). Acceptability of a blended learning model that improves student readiness for practical skill learning: A mixed-methods study. *Focus on Health Professional Education, 17*(1), 3–17. https://doi.org/10.11157/fohpe.v17i1.116

Gardner, P., Slater, H., Jordan, J. E., Fary, R. E., Chua, J., & Briggs, A. M. (2016). Physiotherapy students' perspectives of online e-learning for interdisciplinary management of chronic health conditions: A qualitative study. *BMC Medical Education, 16*(62), 1–9. https://doi.org/10.1186/s12909-016-0593-5

Garrison, D.R. & Vaughan, N.D. (2008). *Blended learning in higher education: Framework, principles, and guidelines.* San Francisco, CA: Jossey-Bass.

Garrison, D. R., Anderson, T., & Archer, W. (2010). The first decade of the community of inquiry framework: A retrospective. *Internet & Higher Education, 13*(1/2), 5–9. http://dx.doi.org/10.1016/j.iheduc.2009.10.003

George, P. P., Papachristou, N., Belisario, J. M., Wang, W., Wark, P. A., Cotic, Z., … Car, J. (2014). Online eLearning for undergraduates in health professions: A systematic review of the impact on knowledge, skills, attitudes and satisfaction. *Journal of Global Health, 4*(1), 1–17. https://doi.org/10.7189/jogh.04.010406

Hayward, L. M. (2004). Integrating web-enhanced instruction into a research methods course: examination of student experiences and perceived learning. *Journal of Physical Therapy Education, 18*(2), 54–65. Retrieved from http://www.aptaeducation.org/members/jopte/index.cfm

Himes, D. O., & Ravert, P. K. (2012). Situated peer coaching and unfolding cases in the fundamentals skills laboratory. *International Journal of Nursing Education Scholarship, 9*(1), 1–19. https://doi.org/10.1515/1548-923X.2335

Huang, T.-C., Huang, Y.-M., & Yu, F.-Y. (2011). Cooperative weblog learning in higher education: Its facilitating effects on social interaction, time lag, and cognitive load. *Educational Technology & Society, 14*(1), 95–106. Retrieved from http://www.ifets.info/journals/14_1/9.pdf

Hurst, K. M. (2016). Using video podcasting to enhance the learning of clinical skills: A qualitative study of physiotherapy students' experi-

ences. *Nurse Education Today, 45*, 206–211. https://doi.org/10.1016/j.nedt.2016.08.011

Kliger, D., & Pfeiffer, E. (2011). Engaging students in blended courses through increased technology. *Journal of Physical Therapy Education, 25*(1), 11–14. Retrieved from http://www.aptaeducation.org/members/jopte/index.cfm

Maloney, S., Storr, M., Morgan, P., & Ilic, D. (2013). The effect of student self-video of performance on clinical skill competency: A randomised controlled trial. *Advances in Health Sciences Education: Theory and Practice, 18*(1), 81–89. http://dx.doi.org/10.1007/s10459-012-9356-1

Maloney, S., Storr, M., Paynter, S., Morgan, P., & Ilic, D. (2013). Investigating the efficacy of practical skill teaching: A pilot-study comparing three educational methods. *Advances in Health Sciences Education: Theory and Practice, 18*(1), 71–80. http://dx.doi.org/10.1007/s10459-012-9355-2

Means, B., Toyama, Y., Murphy, R., & Baki, M. (2013). The effectiveness of online and blended learning: A meta-analysis of the empirical literature. *Teachers College Record, 115*(3), 1–47. Retrieved from http://www.tcrecord.org/content.asp?contentid=16882

Meyer, K. A. (2014). Student engagement in online learning: What works and why. *Association for the Study of Higher Education Higher Education Report, 40*(6), 1–114. https://doi.org/10.1002/aehe.20018

Moore, C., Westwater-Wood, S., & Kerry, R. (2016). Academic performance and perception of learning following a peer coaching teaching and assessment strategy. *Advances in Health Sciences Education: Theory And Practice, 21*(1), 121–130. https://doi.org/10.1007/s10459-015-9618-9

Murray, L., McCallum, C., & Petrosino, C. (2014). Flipping the classroom experience: A comparison of online learning to traditional lecture. *Journal of Physical Therapy Education, 28*(3), 35–41. Retrieved from http://www.aptaeducation.org/members/jopte/index.cfm

Phillips, D., Forbes, H., Duke, M. (2013). Teaching and learning innovations for postgraduate education in nursing. *Collegian, 20*(3), 145–151. https://doi.org/10.1016/j.colegn.2012.05.003

Pittenger, A. A., & Olson-Kellogg, B. (2012). Leveraging learning technologies for collaborative writing in an online pharmacotherapy course. *Distance Education, 33*(1), 61–80. https://doi.org/10.1080/01587919.2012.667960

Preston, E., Ada, L., Dean, C. M., Stanton, R., Waddington, G., & Canning, C. (2012). The Physiotherapy eSkills Training Online resource improves performance of practical skills: a controlled trial. *BMC Medical Education, 12*(119), 1–7. https://doi.org/10.1186/1472-6920-12-119

Rasmussen, K., Belisario, J. M., Wark, P. A., Molina, J. A., Loong, S. L., Cotic, Z., … Car, J. (2014). Offline eLearning for undergraduates in health professions: A systematic review of the impact on knowledge, skills, attitudes and satisfaction. *Journal of Global Health, 4*(1), 0–18. https://doi.org/10.7189/jogh.04.010405

Rowe, M., Bozalek, V., & Frantz, J. (2013). Using Google Drive to facilitate a blended approach to authentic learning. *British Journal of Educational Technology, 44*(4), 594–606. https://doi.org/10.1111/bjet.12063

Stephens, J., & Parr, M. (2013). The development of media-driven clinical skills through using the "e-skills portfolio." *International Journal of Therapy & Rehabilitation, 20*(7), 336–342. https://doi.org/10.12968/ijtr.2013.20.7.336

Tan, S. M., Ladyshewsky, R. R., & Gardner, P. (2010). Using blogging to promote clinical reasoning and metacognition in undergraduate physiotherapy fieldwork programs. *Australasian Journal of Educational Technology, 26*(3), 355–368. https://doi.org/10.14742/ajet.1080

Van Duijn, A. J., Swanick, K., & Donald, E. K. (2014). Student learning of cervical psychomotor skills via online video instruction versus traditional face-to-face instruction. *Journal of Physical Therapy Education, 28*(1), 94–102. Retrieved from http://www.aptaeducation.org/members/jopte/index.cfm

Veneri, D. (2011). The role and effectiveness of computer-assisted learning in physical therapy education: A systematic review. *Physiotherapy Theory & Practice, 27*(4), 287–298. http://dx.doi.org/10.3109/09593985.2010.493192

Veneri, D. A., & Gannotti, M. (2014). A comparison of student outcomes in a physical therapy neurologic rehabilitation course based on delivery mode: Hybrid vs traditional. *Journal of Allied Health, 43*(4), e75–e81. Retrieved from http://www.asahp.org/journal-of-allied-health/

STUDENT PERCEPTIONS OF FACTORS INFLUENCING SUCCESS IN HYBRID AND TRADITIONAL DPT PROGRAMS
A Q-Sort Analysis

Lance Cherry and Mary Blackinton
Nova Southeastern University-Tampa

BACKGROUND AND PURPOSE

Hybrid learning, the blend of online and face-to-face learning experiences, is a novel but rapidly expanding instructional approach in physical therapist education. Our Hybrid Doctor of Physical Therapy (H-DPT) program was designed to provide flexibility for working adults and those with geographic or financial constraints. In the H-DPT Program, students learn via online instruction for 3 weeks followed by 4 days (32-36 hours) of intensive face-to-face learning on-campus each month. During the 3 weeks of online instruction, students watch screen-captured lectures and videos, practice skills, upload videos of themselves performing skills to web-based platforms such as blogs, receive feedback from peers and faculty, take quizzes, read texts, and submit assignments related to course content. Most learning activities occur at self-selected times asynchronously, although there are occa-sional synchronous activities such as web-based meetings. All courses have weekly deadlines for assignments and quizzes. The 4 days of face-to-face instruction consists of psychomotor skill practice accompanied by immediate feedback, honing clinical reasoning and problem-solving skills, applying material learned in lecture-based courses (debates, journal clubs), and taking high-stakes practical and written exams.

Garrison and Vaughan (2008) refer to blended learning as the "thoughtful fusion of online and face-to-face experiences" (p. 5). Hybrid instruction is a distinct instructional modality. It is distinct from traditional classrooms, where all instruction is done face to face; it is different than online courses, where all instruction is done online: and it is dissimilar to "flipped" classrooms, where there is a shift in passive learning activities (lectures) to online while bringing application (case studies) into the classroom (Berrett, 2012;

• **Lance Cherry**, Associate Professor, Department of Physical Therapy, Nova Southeastern University-Tampa, 3632 Queen Palm Drive, Tampa, FL 33619. Telephone: (813) 574-5327. E-mail: lc1315@nova.edu

The Quarterly Review of Distance Education, Volume 18(4), 2017, pp. 71–81
ISSN 1528-3518

Boucher, Robertson, Wainner, & Sanders, 2013; Murray, McCallum, & Petrosino, 2014; Wong & Chu, 2014). While some researchers evaluated factors influencing student success or retention in online and blended environments (Smith, 2005; Smith, Murphy, & Mahoney, 2003), none to date have investigated factors impacting success in hybrid DPT programs. It is also unclear if there are differences in student perceptions regarding what factors impact student success in traditional versus hybrid DPT programs.

Academic success can be viewed through a variety of lenses. Alexander Astin (2012) suggests that student outcomes (O) are a result of "inputs" (I) or personal qualities that students bring to the educational experience (academic achievement, study behaviors, aspiration, financial status, life goals), as well as "environment" (E) factors that the students experience during the academic experience (program policies, curriculum, facilities, instructors, friends, family support, teaching styles). This "IEO" model reflects the milieu of factors impacting student outcomes.

Similarly, Rovai's persistence model in distance education distinguishes pre-admission variables such as student characteristics (academic preparation, age, ethnicity) and student skills (computer literacy, time management) from post-admission variables such as learning community, interpersonal relationships, study habits, advising, teaching/learning styles, finances, hours of employment, and family responsibilities (Rovai, 2003). In physical therapy education, predictors of academic success have been analyzed using student inputs prior to and during the professional curriculum such as grade point average and standardized exam scores (Kosmahl, 2005), as well as program variables such as accreditation status, number of faculty with PhD or EdD degrees, and total years of preprofessional and professional coursework (Mohr, Ingram, Hayes, & Du, 2005).

In the context of blended learning environments, Garrison and Vaughan (2008) describe a community of inquiry framework depicting factors that influence learning in blended classrooms. This framework describes three realms influencing student learning in the hybrid classroom: social presence, cognitive presence, and teaching presence. Social presence refers to the personal communication and camaraderie between students and between students and faculty; cognitive presence is the exploration and exchange of information and new ideas; and teaching presence refers to the educational design, direction, and focus created by the instructor (Garrison & Vaughan, 2008). These elements, in addition to those variables put forth by Astin and Rovai, suggest there are many variables that could influence student success in a hybrid DPT program.

Student perceptions of variables impacting success have been investigated in health professions education, although not related to online or hybrid programs specifically. A qualitative study investigated factors influencing academic achievement in high achieving medical students (Abdulghani et al., 2014). Using focus groups and grounded theory analysis, the researchers identified four primary themes related to academic success: learning strategies, resource management, motivation, and dealing with nonacademic problems (Abdulghani et al., 2014). These four themes were further broken down into 17 subthemes, such as lecture attendance, prioritization of learning needs, mind mapping, and learning from mistakes (learning strategy theme), time management and family support (resource management theme), internal motivation and exam results (motivation), and language barriers, homesickness, and stress (dealing with non-academic problem theme).

Similarly, student perceptions of dental school including morale, strengths and challenges, and ranking of content area importance were researched using a survey of students from five western dental schools (Cardall, 2008). The findings from over 740 student participants revealed the top five positive influences on their school experience included faculty, clinical experiences, classmates, curriculum, and facilities; whereas the most frequent negative experiences related to curriculum, clinical experience, organization, student/faculty ratio, and patient pool (Cardall, 2008). Interestingly, clinical experience and the curriculum were viewed as both positive and negative influences.

In summary, there is a dearth of literature in physical therapy education regarding factors students believe to influence success, and little to no literature describing such beliefs related to hybrid education in the health professions or specific to physical therapy.

The overarching purpose of this investigation was to determine students' perceptions of factors they believe influence their success in a hybrid DPT program and to compare their perceptions with students in a traditional DPT program. Understanding students' beliefs about success is analogous to understanding patients' health beliefs. By identifying student perceptions about success, programs can potentially identify potential barriers and facilitators in designing hybrid classrooms and curricula, improve the admissions selection process to better match applicants with the hybrid program, share findings with prospective applicants to improve their understanding of the program, and assist faculty who advise students.

METHODOLOGY

Subjects

Following institutional review board approval, subjects were recruited from two programs within one university—a hybrid DPT program and a traditional DPT program. Students were recruited verbally and via email. No incentives or rewards were provided to participants.

Identification of Variables

Based on a review of the literature regarding students' perception of success in online/ hybrid education and in health professions

education, we identified variables potentially impacting student success (Rovai, 2003; Park & Choi, 2009; Smith, 2005; Smith et al., 2005). Our goal was to include variables related to both the individual student (I) and educational environment (E) as described in Astin's work. We also wanted to ensure that E variables reflected all areas the community of inquiry model (Garrison & Vaughan, 2008) for hybrid learning: social, instructor, and cognitive presence. Three faculty reviewed the variables for face validity, and as a result 36 variables were identified (Table 1).

Q-Sort Survey Methodology

Since this study was conducted to investigate student perceptions of success, we used a descriptive methodology called Q-Sort because it characterizes opinions through comparative rank ordering (Portney & Watkins, 2015). According to Dennis (1986), Q-Sort is particularly valuable in research that explores human perceptions and interpersonal relationships. The Q-Sort procedure requires participants to sort a set of items (in this case, 36 factors influencing their success) into five ordinal categories, ranging from most influential to least influential, regarding student success. The number of items permitted in each category is fixed in advance so the shape of the distribution of item scores is constant for all students and reflects a bell-shaped curve.

Procedures

To begin the Q-Sort, each participant received a set of 36 index cards, each index card describing one variable that potentially influenced student success. Participants were not given an operational definition of success, and if they asked, were told, "whatever you feel is success as a student. Participants were provided a symmetrical bell-shaped grid on poster board consisting of columns numbered one through five; each column representing a different degree of influencing student success (Figure 1). Column 1 was labeled "least influ-

TABLE 1

Student Variables Identified Through Literature Review
and Organized by Astin's IEO Model and the Community of Inquiry Model

Individual Student Characteristics		Educational Characteristics		
Student Attributes/ Skills	Student External Variables	Social Presence	Instructor Presence	Cognitive Presence
• Academic work ethic • Beliefs about teaching and learning • Self-confidence in learning • Self-initiative in learning • Prior academic performance (grades) • Preadmission major (study area) • Previous work experience • Ability to filter large amounts of information • Ability to prioritize study focus • Computer literacy • Ability to search information online • Time management • Reading skills • Writing skills • Problem-solving skills	• Finances • Hours worked per week • Family demands • Outside support and encouragement • Life crises	• Collaboration with peers online • Collaboration with peers face to face • Access to student services • Social peer interaction • Peer support	• Instructor responsiveness to student needs • Instructor's ability to foster a sense of community • Instructor's ability to organize course material • Instructor's ability to clarify course/ assignment expectations • The frequency of instructor interaction • Timeliness of information from instructor • Timeliness of feedback from the instructor	• Degree to which class activities aid reflection and learning • Organization of courses in the curriculum • Types of available course resources (books, videos) • Access to resources outside the classroom (library, physical therapist)

ential," column 2 "not very influential," column 3 "somewhat influential," column 4 "very influential," and column 5 "most influential." To maintain a bell-shaped curve suggested for Q-Sort methodology, participants were limited in the number of cards they could place under each column: 4 cards for "most" and "least" influential, 8 cards in "not very" and "very" influential, and 12 cards in the "somewhat influential" column (Figure 1). Participants were instructed to take as much time as they needed to complete the Q-Sort, placing all 36 cards (variables) in each column as they saw fit. They were also told that the order of the cards (variables) within each column did not matter, just the selection of which column to place each variable. As students finished, they

notified the PI or coinvestigator, who then double-checked that all the spaces were filled and no cards were left over.

In order to maintain the appropriate groups for proper data input, the cards from each column were placed in a corresponding envelope marked 1–5. When all cards were placed in envelopes from a particular students' board they were wrapped together with a rubber band and placed in a larger envelope until they were input for data analysis.

Data Analysis

The Q-Sort analysis looks for correlations between subjects across a sample of variables

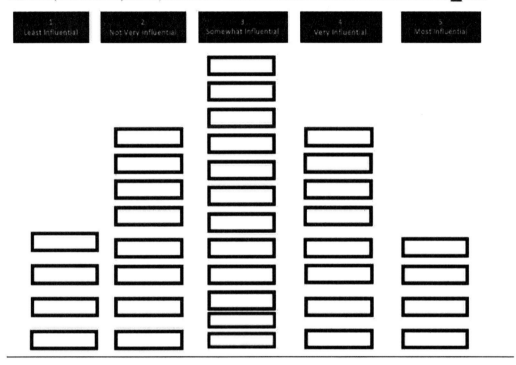

FIGURE 1
Q-Sort Directions

(Portney & Watkins, 2009), reducing many individual viewpoints of the subjects down to a few factors. The term *factor* in the Q-Sort is defined as representing individuals with similar views, feelings, or experiences (Akhtar-Danesh et al., 2013). In our Q-sort, factors represent groups of individuals with similar views about which variables influenced student success.

For this study, analysis of the Q-Sorts was conducted using the PQ Method 2.33, a free downloadable software program (Schmolck, 2014). This is the program most recommended by the International Society for the Scientific Study of Subjectivity. The PQ Method is a statistical program tailored to the requirements of Q-Sort studies. Specifically, it allows the user to enter each Q-Sort individually, identifying which variables were selected in each of the 5 columns. The PQ Method program computes intercorrelations among Q-Sort, which are then factor analyzed and rotated for simplification (Schmolck, 2012). The analysis step produces an extensive report with a variety of tables on factor loadings, statement factor scores, and discriminating statements for each of the factors (Schmolck, 2012).

The number of factors created by the Q-Sort program is based on a correlation matrix between all Q-Sorts followed by factor matrix analysis. Each factor thus had its own set of scores, expressed as z scores for each variable/statement. Since there so many variables represented in each factor, we reported each factor using only those variables with z scores greater than or equal to 1.5 (representing most influential) and less than or equal to -1.5 (representing least influential). The individual statement factor z scores were used to develop an understanding of the profile for each factor and to make comparisons among the factors.

This Q-Sort methodology cannot compare two different data sets (hybrid vs. traditional) directly as one might do in an independent t test. Instead, we entered the data for the H-DPT program and DPT program separately and compared the factors identified by each group.

RESULTS

Two cohorts completed the Q-Sort: Hybrid DPT Students (H-DPT) and Traditional DPT students (DPT). Results for each Q-Sort are reported separately based on the way the Q-sorts were analyzed.

Hybrid DPT Students

Participants. A total of 54 H-DPT students participated, including 20 second-year students and 34 first-year students. Although demographic data were not collected, the average age of the two cohorts combined (based on admission statistics) was 26.2 years, 58% female and 42% male.

Factors. The Q-Sort data from the Hybrid sample created four factors. Again, a factor is a subgroup of responses representing groups of individuals with similar views about which variables influenced student success ranked in a similar manner using correlations. For each of the four factors, the statements with z scores of greater than +1.5 ("strongly impacting success") or less than -1.5 ("least impacting success") are identified (Table 2). Among the statements with z scores of greater than +1.5 (most influencing success), "self-initiation in learning" was identified in all four factors, and "time management" noted in three of the four factors, whereas "academic work ethic" and "student ability to identify study focus" were identified in two of the four factors (Table 2). Among the statements with z scores of less than -1.5 (least influencing student success), "access to student services" was identified in

three of the four factors, and "beliefs about teaching and learning" was identified in two of the four factors (Table 2).

Consensus Statements. The Q-Sort program identified consensus statements, meaning those statements that did not significantly distinguish one group (factor) from any other group (factor). For the Hybrid program, there were six consensus statements (Table 3). There were three positive consensus statements (students perceived it strongly impacted success) including: "self-initiative in learning," "problem-solving skills, and "organization of courses in the curriculum." There were also three negative consensus statements (students perceived it did not impact success) including: "prior academic performance," "writing skills" and "access to resources outside the classroom."

Traditional DPT Students

Participants. Seventy-one traditional DPT students participated in the Q-Sort. Although demographic data were not collected, the average age of the two cohorts combined (based on admission statistics) was 24.3 years. Gender was not identified in the traditional cohort.

Factors. The Q-Sort data from the Traditional sample created four factors. For traditional students, "time management" was identified as strongly influencing success in three of the four factors, while "academic work ethic" and "ability to prioritize study focus" were identified in two of the four factors. The statement with the highest positive z score for the traditional group was "instructor's ability to organize course material."

In the Traditional sample, there was little similarity between the four factors in the statements ranked as "least influential" for impacting student success. "Access to student services" was identified by two of the four factors as being among the least influential. No other statements were similar across factors; however, statements with the highest negative z scores were: "hours worked per week," "finances," and "preadmission major."

TABLE 2
Hybrid Student Factors and Perceptions Rated Most and Least Likely to Impact Success*

Factor	1	2	3	4
# Defining variables	9	9	10	4
Composite reliability coefficient	.97	.97	.98	.94
SE Z scores	.164	.164	.156	.243
Variables most impacting success (z score)	• Self-initiation in learning (1.98) • Ability to prioritize study focus (1.80) • Academic work ethic (1.76) • Time management (1.69)	• Time management (2.2) • Self-initiation in learning (1.78) • Ability to prioritize study focus (1.51)	• Self-initiative in learning (1.81) • Degree class aids reflection and learning (1.65) • Academic work ethic (1.50)	• Time management (1.67) • Instructors ability clarify expectations (1.63) • Self-initiative in learning (1.57)
Variables least impacting success (z score)	• Preadmission major (−1.89) • Finances (−1.80) • Access to student services (−1.57)	• Access to student services (−2.12) • Beliefs about teaching/learning (−1.91)	• Family demands (-2.11) • Beliefs about teaching/ learning (−1.76) • Access to student services (−1.62)	• Instructors ability to foster a sense of community (−2.26) • Social peer interaction (−2.06)

Note: *Based on z scores ±1.5 standard deviations.

TABLE 3
Hybrid Student Consensus Statements

Positive Consensus Statements	Negative Consensus Statements
• Self-initiative in learning • Problem-solving skills • Organization of courses in the curriculum	• Prior academic performance (grades) • Writing skills • Access to resources outside the classroom

Consensus Statements. Again, consensus statements are those statements that did not significantly distinguish one group (factor) from any other group (factor). For the traditional group, there were no consensus statements within the four factors, either positive or negative.

DISCUSSION

The purpose of this study was to determine students' perceptions of factors they believe influence their success in a hybrid DPT program and to compare their perceptions with students in a traditional DPT program. The Q-Sort methodology required participants to rank order the most and least important attributes related to their success, forcing them to consider all attributes potentially related to success rather than selecting a single attribute as one might do in survey methodology. In this discussion, factors represent groups of individuals with similar views about which variables influenced student success. The H-DPT and DPT student Q-Sorts were analyzed separately based on the capability of the PQ Method 2.33.

TABLE 4
Traditional Student Factors and Perceptions Rated Most and Least Likely to Impact Success

Factor	1	2	3	4
# Defining variables	19	15	9	6
Composite reliability Coefficient	.99	.98	.97	.96
SE Z scores	.114	.128	.164	.200
Variables most impacting success (z score)	• Time management (2.10) • Academic work ethic (1.50)	• Time management (2.07) • Ability to prioritize study focus (1.94)	• Time management (1.95) • Academic work ethic (1.72) • Problem-solving skills (1.69) • Ability to prioritize study focus (1.61)	• Instructor's ability to organize course material (2.19) • Instructor responsiveness to student needs (1.71)
Variables least impacting success (z score)	• Hours worked/week (−2.07) • Finances (−1.97)	• Access to student services (−1.86) • Collaboration with peers online (−1.70)	• Prior academic performance (−1.63) • Social peer interaction (−1.63) • Previous work experience (−1.56)	• Preadmission major (−1.82) • Access to student services (−1.51) • Writing skills (−1.50) • Instructor's ability to foster community (−1.50)

Note: *Based on z scores ±1.5 standard deviations.

There were several differences between the hybrid and traditional DPT student perceptions. Self-initiation in learning was identified in all four factor groups in the Hybrid program, with z scores ranging from 1.57–1.98; whereas it was not included in any of the four factor groups from the Traditional program. This finding was not surprising, given the nature of hybrid instruction. Although self-directed learning is a characteristic of professionalism in physical therapy (May, Morgan, Lemke, Karst, & Stone, 1995) students in a hybrid program must be self-directed to independently navigate the learning experiences during the online portion of each month. For example, in most traditional programs, students attend classes at set times each week, following the pace of learning set by the instructor. In contrast, students in a hybrid program access online lectures and videos at self-selected times and a self-selected pace. Further, in our hybrid program, students have weekly assignments to keep them engaged and must then be self-directed to complete the assignments on time.

Another difference between the hybrid and traditional DPT students' perceptions of success was the perceived role of the instructor. In the traditional DPT cohort, one of the four factor groups included "instructor's ability to organize course material," whereas none of the four factor groups in the H-DPT program included this variable. In fact, the highest z score for the traditional DPT students across all factor groups was this variable. Although it was only a factor in one traditional DPT factor group, it may indicate that some traditional DPT students perceive the instructor's organizational skills in organizing class material as being more important than their own attributes.

In contrast, three of the four factor groups in both the Hybrid and Traditional students identified time management as a variable strongly impacting success. Given the intensive nature of physical therapist education, this was not surprising. These findings are like those reported by Abdulghani et al. (2014) in medical students. It is possible that the reasons why time management was rated as strongly influencing success may be different between students in each program. For example, most hybrid DPT students juggle work/family along with school demands, while the traditional students manage a more-intensive course load and must be on-campus every day. Time management is an attribute however that all DPT students emphasized, and this should be shared with prospective students in all programs.

Two variables, "academic work ethic" and "ability to prioritize study focus" were identified as strongly impacting success by two of the four factor groups in both cohorts. These findings are similar to prior research for online learning identified study habits as an important post-admission variable impacting student retention (Rovai, 2003; Smith, 2005).

Consensus statements are those statements that did not significantly distinguish one group (factor) from any other group (factor). Interestingly, the Hybrid cohort had six consensus statements while the Traditional cohort had none. One reason for this difference might be the shared experience of being in a hybrid DPT program. While all students have had similar experiences in traditional classrooms, few students in the Hybrid program had previous exposure to hybrid learning. The uniqueness of being in a hybrid program may have more strongly shaped their perceptions related to what it takes to be successful. For example, DPT students in traditional programs use the same learning strategies they've employed prior to PT school, whereas hybrid DPT students were potentially forced to develop new or different strategies. Further, their experience was unusual or different than most other

professional programs, and so they may be more aware or reflective of factors impacting success.

The three consensus statements rated as strongly related to success in all hybrid factor groups included: self-initiative in learning, problem-solving skills, and organization of courses in the curriculum. As stated previously, the importance of self-initiation as an attribute makes sense in a hybrid curriculum because students must organize, plan, and engage in learning on their own time frame. Problem-solving may have been rated consistently high across all factor groups for several reasons. First, the technology itself is an area in which students must problem-solve in online and hybrid environments (Kowalczyk, 2014; Stott & Moser, 2016; Talcott, O'Donnell, & Burns, 2013). For example, in the hybrid program, students must create and upload videos demonstrating a psychomotor skill, and can encounter problems uploading the video in a correct file format to the course management system. It is also possible that time management issues, clearly identified in this study, require problem-solving to decide how to prioritize study and work time. Also, in the H-DPT program, students have more graded assignments than in the Traditional program. When students encounter questions about the assignment or pertaining to the lecture, they are free to contact faculty; however, many first try to problem-solve on their own before emailing or calling faculty. This is different than being in a classroom where students can raise their hand and easily get a question answered.

There are several limitations of this study. First, the population from which the sample was drawn represents only those students in one university, albeit two distinct programs, so findings cannot be generalized to other programs. Second, students volunteered to participate in the study, meaning they may be those individuals with stronger feelings/perceptions about factors that influence success. Third, the H-DPT program was only in its second year, and it is possible that the perceptions of students would be different in a more mature, stable program. As the program matured, instructional practices became more sophisticated and consistent than they were in the first 2 years of the program. Last, the definition of "student success" was not operationally defined for the participants, because it was the authors' intentions to allow students to self-select their perception of success. This may have led to a lack of uniformity in analyzing variables impacting success.

Suggestions for future research include the following: (1) replicate the Q-Sort in the H-DPT program to see if student perceptions have changed now that the program is more mature; (2) conduct a qualitative study to probe students lived experiences in the H-DPT program regarding the variables identified in this study; (3) compare student perceptions in the first versus final year of the program; (4) compare student perceptions between those students in the top versus bottom quartile measured by final grade point average.

CONCLUSION

While both hybrid and traditional students perceive time management, academic work ethic, and ability to prioritize study focus as strongly influencing student success, self-initiation in learning, problem-solving, and organization of courses were perceived by only H-DPT students as factors influencing success whereas the instructor's ability to organize course material was only identified by the traditional DPT students. Further, there was consensus in the H-DPT cohort regarding factors influencing success compared to traditional DPT students.

Author Note: This article was also published in Volume 14, Issue 4 of *Distance Learning*.

REFERENCES

Akhtar-Danesh, N., Baumann, A., Kolotylo, C., Lawlor, Y., Tompkins, C., & Lee, R. (2013). Perceptions of professionalism among nursing faculty and nursing students. *Western Journal of Nursing Research, 35*(2), 248–271.

Abdulghani, H. M., Abdulmajeed, A. A., Khalil, M. S., Ahmad, F., Ponnamperuma, G. G., & Amin, Z. (2014). What factors determine academic achievement in high achieving undergraduate medical students? A qualitative study. *Medical Teacher, 36*, S43–S48.

Astin, A. W., & Antonio, A. L. (2012). *Assessment for excellence: The philosophy and practice of assessment and evaluation in higher education* (2nd ed.). Lanham, MD. Rowman & Littlefield.

Berrett, D. (2012, February 19). How "flipping" the classroom can improve the traditional lecture. *The Chronicle of Higher Education, 58*(25), A16–A18.

Boucher, B., Robertson, E., Wainner, R., & Sanders B. (2013). "Flipping" Texas State University's physical therapist musculoskeletal curriculum: Implementation of a hybrid learning model. *Journal of Physical Therapy Education, 27*(3), 72–77.

Cardall, W. R., Rowan, R.C., & Bay, C. (2008). Dental education from the students' perspective: Curriculum and climate. *Journal of Dental Education, 72*(5), 600–609.

Dennis, K. E. (1986). Q-methodology: Relevance and application to nursing research. *Advances in Nursing Science, 8*, 6–17.

Garrison, D. R., & Vaughan, N. D. (2008). *Blended learning in higher education: Framework, principles, and guidelines.* San Francisco, CA: Jossey-Bass.

Kosmahl, E. M. (2005). Factors related to physical therapist license examination scores. *Journal of Physical Therapy Education, 19*(2), 52–56.

Kowalczyk, N. K. (2014). *Perceived barriers to online education by radiologic science educators. Radiologic Technology, 85*(5), 486–493.

May, W. W., Morgan, B. J., Lemke, J. C., Karst, G. M., & Stone, H. L. (1995). Model for ability-based assessment in physical therapy education. *Journal of Physical Therapy Education, 9*(1), 3–6.

Mohr, T., Ingram, D., Hayes, S., & Du, Z. (2005). Educational program characteristics and pass rates on the National Physical Therapy Examination. *Journal of Physical Therapy Education, 19*(1), 60–66.

Murray, L., McCallum, C., & Petrosino, C. (2014). Flipping the classroom experience: A comparison of online learning to traditional lecture.

Journal of Physical Therapy Education, 28(3), 35–41.

Park, J., & Choi, H. J. (2009). Factors influencing adult learners' decision to drop or persist in online learning. *Educational Technology and Society, 12*(4), 207–214.

Portney, L. G., Watkins, M. P. (2015). *Foundations of clinical research: Applications to practice* (3rd ed.). Philadelphia, PA: F. A. Davis.

Rovai, A. P. (2003). In search of higher persistence rates in distance education online programs. *Internet and Higher Education, 6*, 1–16.

Schmolck, P. (2012). PQ Method (Version 2.33, adapted from mainframe-program Qmethod written by John Atkinson, 1992) [Computer Software]. Munich, Germany: Bundeswehr University of Munich. Retrieved from http://www.lrz-muenchen.de/~schmolck/qmethod/downpqx.htm

Schmolck, P. (2014). The PQ Method manual. Retrieved from the PQ Method website: http://schmolck.userweb.mwn.de/qmethod/pqmanual.htm

Smith, P. J. (2005). Learning preferences and readiness for online learning. *Educational Psychology, 25*(1), 3–12.

Smith, P. J., Murphy K. L., Mahoney, S. E. (2003). Towards identifying factors underlying readiness for online learning: An exploratory study. *Distance Education, 24*(1), 57–67.

Stott, A., & Mozer, M. (2016). Connecting learners online: Challenges and issues for nurse education—Is there a way forward? *Nurse Education Today, 39*, 152–154.

Talcott, K. S., O'Donnell, J. M., & Burns, H. K. (2013). Overcoming barriers in online workshop development: An ELITE experience. *Journal of Continuing Education in Nursing, 44*(6), 264–268.

Wong K., & Chu, D. W. K. (2014). Is the flipped classroom model effective in the perspectives of students' perceptions and benefits? In S. K. S. Cheung, J. Fong, J. Zhang, R. Kwan, & L. F. Kwok (Eds.), *Hybrid learning theory and practice, Proceedings of the 7th International Conference ICHL 2014, Shanghai, China* (pp. 93–104). New York, NY: Springer.

CONFERENCE CALENDAR

Charles Schlosser
Nova Southeastern University

The following conferences may be of interest to the readers of the *Quarterly Review of Distance Education.*

ISTE, June 24–27, Chicago, IL

"ISTE 2018 is the place where educator-tested strategies come together with proven resources for transforming learning and teaching. It's also the place to get connected to the brightest minds in edtech, then network with them all year long."
http://conference.iste.org/2018/

EdMedia, June 25–29, Amsterdam, The Netherlands

"EdMedia + Innovate Learning, the premier international conference in the field since 1987, spans all disciplines and levels of education attracting researchers and practitioners in the field from 70+ countries. This annual conference offers a forum for the discussion and exchange of research, development, and applications on all topics related to innovation and education.
https://www.aace.org/conf/edmedia/

Distance Teaching & Learning Conference, August 7–9, Madison, WI

"DT&L isn't just a conference, it's a community of educators with ideas and experiences to share. You'll laugh, you'll be moved, and you'll come away with new ways to approach your work and put research into practice. You'll meet people who can help your career thrive. You'll also get to enjoy Madison—a walkable, culture-filled city nestled between two beautiful lakes. It's the perfect place to learn, explore, and relax this summer."
https://dtlconference.wisc.edu/

E-Learn World Conference on E-Learning, October 15–18, Las Vegas, NV

"E-Learn World Conference on E-Learning is an international conference organized by the AACE-Association for the Advancement of Computing in Education and cosponsored by the *International Journal on E-Learning.* E-Learn provides a unique forum for government, healthcare, education, and business professionals to discuss the latest research,

• **Charles Schlosser**, Adjunct Associate Professor, Fischler College of Education, Nova Southeastern University, 3301 College Avenue, Fort Lauderdale, FL 33314. E-mail: charles.schlosser@nova.edu

The Quarterly Review of Distance Education, Volume 18(3), 2017, p. 83   ISSN 1528-3518
Copyright © 2017 Information Age Publishing, Inc.   All rights of reproduction in any form reserved.

development, applications, issues, and strategies, to explore new technologies, and to identify solutions for today's challenges related to online learning. A variety of opportunities and venues are designed to enable participants to actively learn from and collaborate with a multinational, cross-industry expert faculty and peers on the research, development, diverse learning experiences, implementation and technology needed to improve e-learning."
https://www.aace.org/conf/elearn/

AECT International Convention, October 23–27, Kansas City, MO

"The AECT International Convention brings together participants from around the world, offering practical applications, cutting-edge research, hands-on workshops, and demonstrations of new technologies in teaching and learning. Take this opportunity to connect with your peers! The goal of the convention is for participants from around the world to learn from the experiences and activities of the convention, enriching their professional lives."
http://members.aect.org/events/call/

Future of Education Technology Conference (FETC), January 27-30, 2019, Orlando, FL

"For nearly 40 years, the Future of Education Technology Conference has gathered the most dynamic and creative education professionals from around the world for an intensive, highly collaborative exploration of new technologies, best practices and pressing issues. Its impact has been felt by thousands of districts, schools, educators—and ultimately students. Each year, FETC is tailored to the needs of an increasingly technology-driven education community—and 2019 will be no exception. The 39th National Future of Education Technology Conference features industry experts and unrivaled agenda content, an Expo Hall filled with the latest and greatest solutions, and a community of thousands eager to network with like-minded peers. Your colleagues at FETC may come with different experiences and expertise, but they share your challenges and goals. School and district administrators, classroom teachers, information professionals, special education directors, curriculum and media specialists, and other educators with roles or interest in ed tech, attend FETC year after year to find the professional learning, technology solutions and connections they need to transform learning in and out of the classroom. Join them for four days of collaboration, innovation and learning, and discover new ways to spark change with technology."
http://www.fetc.org/

AUTHOR BIOGRAPHICAL DATA

Ayshah Alahmari is a doctoral candidate in teaching and learning at Illinois State University-Normal. She was born and raised in Saudi Arabia and has more than 10 years of teaching experience in Saudi schools. She had been granted two scholarships from the Ministry of Education in Saudi Arabia to pursue master's and doctorate degrees in teaching and learning at Illinois State University. She has collaborated on scholarly projects and publications about e-learning and online education in Saudi Arabia. Her research interests include e-Learning, blended learning, m-learning, online education, collaborative learning, technology integration, and online teacher professional development. Her current research examines the impact of using collaborative technology tools to enhance collaborative learning in online learning environments.

Ray J. Amirault is a graduate of Florida State University's Instructional Systems Program and currently serves as an instructional technologist in the College of Education Office of the Dean at Illinois State University.

Mary Blackinton, PT, EdD, GCS, is the director of the DPT Program at Nova Southeastern University-Tampa, a completely blended entry-level doctor of physical therapy program that started in 2011. She received her BS degree in physical therapy from University of Maryland, a MS in gerontology from Nova University, and an EdD in health care education from Nova Southeastern University. She has been a faculty member at Nova Southeastern University since 1994, serving as director of the Transition DPT Program from 2002 to 2010. Blackinton's educational research interests focus on the scholarship of teaching and learning. She is the cochair of the Health Professions Educational Research Symposium (www.nova.edu/hpers). Along with the DPT faculty at NSU-Tampa, she was coinvestigator of a grant entitled: "Where does the time go? A work sampling study comparing faculty activities in traditional and hybrid DPT Programs." She was also a coinvestigator for "A tale of 2 case methods: Investigating the student learning outcomes of two teaching strategies designed to enhance clinical reasoning." She has been the dissertation chair for five PhD graduates and is a reviewer for the following journals: *Journal of Physical Therapy Education* and *Journal of Neurologic Physical Therapy*. Her article entitled "Teaching an Hands-on Profession in an Online Classroom" was published in *Physical Therapy in Motion* (November, 2013). Blackinton is a director at large for the American Council of Academic Physical Therapy.

Lance Cherry, MPT, EdD, OCS, received his BS from the University of Florida, his master of physical therapy from Emory University, and his EdD in applied physiology from Teachers College, Columbia University. He is board certified in orthopedic physical therapy and is presently an associate professor in the doctor of physical therapy program at Nova

The Quarterly Review of Distance Education, Volume 18(4), 2017, pp. 85–86
Copyright © 2017 Information Age Publishing, Inc.
ISSN 1528-3518

Southeastern University-Tampa. Cherry teaches courses in musculoskeletal physical therapy and differential diagnosis in a hybrid format. His scholarship focuses on use of hybrid instructional strategies in health care education as well as student attrition.

Ray Kalinski has a PhD in organization and management and has taught in the MBA program at Kaplan University for about 9 years. His masters is in education from the University of Nebraska. He has 30+ years' experience in the aerospace industry where he has held positions in information system's management, operations, and shared services.

Melissa Lazinski, PT, DPT, OCS, received her doctor of physical therapy from Regis University and her bachelor of health science in physical therapy from the University of Florida. She is board certified in orthopedic physical therapy. She is an associate professor at the doctor of physical therapy program of Nova Southeastern University-Tampa Campus. Lazinski teaches courses in musculoskeletal physical in a hybrid format. Her scholarship focuses on use of hybrid instructional strategies in health care education.

Joel Olson has a PhD in human resources from Colorado State University, Ft. Collins and an MA in theology from Denver Seminary. He has 20 years experience in nonprofit leadership and consultation, education, and instructional design. Most recently, he has served the Reformed Church in America and the Evangelical Presbyterian Church as a consultant for churches in crisis. Currently he serves as a human resources professor in the School of Business and Management at Purdue University Global.

Sherrill Waddell taught English in Florida's Broward and Palm Beach counties before moving to Texas, where she worked in middle, high, and alternative schools, as well as juvenile correctional facilities. She worked with the University of Texas to launch the LUCHA Program in her district so non-English speaking students could enroll in online courses for credit in their native language. She then moved to the online sector and worked as a manager and master teacher for Connections Education. She is currently working on writing a book about education.

CPSIA information can be obtained
at www.ICGtesting.com
Printed in the USA
FFOW01n1436180618
47172019-49818FF